AF390654

January 2024 (English version)
March 2023 (French version: ISBN 978-2-9582456-2-7)

# Brief Solutions to Philosophical Problems
## Using a Hegelian Method

Publishing both essays and fiction, Éditions Skhedia remains philosophical insofar as it addresses the questions that underlie all others. To go through them, the precariousness of the human craft is inevitable – we have only a raft (skhedia, in Greek), as Plato suggests in the *Phaedo*. Keeping this in mind urges us to avoid all purely gratuitous questions, replacing them with those that engage the existence of the questioner. We need to be aware of the mysteries and perils that surround us to understand how *vital* the exercise of thought is. Each book in this publishing house attempts, in its own way, this journey that is as uncertain as it is necessary.

# Brief Solutions to Philosophical Problems Using a Hegelian Method

Léonor FRANC

# Brief Solutions to Philosophical Problems
# Using a Hegelian Method

Éditions σχεδία

"Contradiction is the rule of truth." [1]

Hegel

---

[1]"Contradictio est regula veri." Extract from Hegel's defense of his habilitation thesis at Jena in 1801. *Werke (Frühe Schriften)*, vol. 1, Frankfurt, Suhrkamp, 1986, p. 533.

## Solution 1

The first question in any search for truth must be: is there anything to talk about? Because if there is not, there is no point in even starting a search.

The answer here lies in the question. There is at least one question, there is at least this thought that questions. At this stage, there may be no human body, no sun, no air, no matter, but there is at least this thought that expresses this doubt. Such is the *cogito* presented by Descartes, surely inspired by Augustine. With the *cogito*, we are not dealing with a demonstrated result; otherwise, we would be asking for the demonstration of that demonstration, and so on *ad infinitum*. If we ask "Why the *cogito*?" we might reply "Because 'Why the *cogito*?'," i.e., the individual answers the question simply by asking it. To question the *cogito* is to think, and thus reinforces the intuition of the truth of the *cogito*. Doubt annihilates itself. What is the cause of the *cogito*? the *cogito* itself. What is truly the cause of itself is neither the universe nor God nor the concept of substance, but the *cogito*.

A somewhat narrow-minded individual could, of course, question the question, then question the question of the question, and so on, and thus warn of a dangerous infinite regress of "proofs." Eventually, however, he will notice that this questioning can be duplicated ad infinitum without ever ceasing to be a thought. This individual will come to realize that the very act of asking a question reinforces the *cogito*, and that his question will always be a question, even if it contains billions of layers of doubt. The "infinite regress" shown here simply reveals the *infinite truth* of the *cogito*.

Scholium

We cannot answer the question of what would happen if thought stopped – which is sometimes assimilated to death, but also corresponds, less tragically, to a dreamless sleep, or an unconscious or forgotten thought. Is there any other way to relate to the world and ourselves than through thought? What happens to a thought when it is forgotten? We cannot know, because if we knew it, it would not be forgotten. The question itself is a false question, a question that does not know what it is asking. We note not only our inability to answer this question, but also our inability to ask it – so this scholium should not even be written.

To rephrase it in vain a second and final time: we cannot understand what the cessation of thought would consist of, since we would be thinking about this cessation. *A fortiori*, we cannot be sure that it exists[2], since we do not even know what it might consist of. We cannot pass any judgment on this. Anything claimed about the cessation of thought would be unverifiable; we could not even verify that such a statement is referring to the cessation of thought.

This scholium only reminds us that the unverifiable is always possible. We could try (but it can only be an attempt) to put it this way: one day the world may have "-10 dimensions," or it is possible that one day ⊥꒦ᴄ⅄ᖚ.

---

[2] As far as we are, we are even sure that this cessation or nothingness cannot exist, as we will see in more detail later.

# Scholium 2

The phenomena we generally associate with the "unconscious" are in fact expressions of the involuntary, which is something very different. It is true that certain thoughts "come to us," "come back to our mind," and so on. On the question of whether we have self-mastery or not, it will be necessary to read the solution on freedom.

## Solution 2

We now have to ask ourselves what exactly we have found with the *cogito*. The *cogito* is a thought, but what is a thought? Does the world exist beyond this thought? Have we "only" found thought? What about the reality of *what* we think? This is the classic problem of realism and idealism, of the objective and the subjective, of the existence or non-existence of something external to the human mind.

Berkeley has shown us that there is nothing external to the mind. In fact, if we tried to think of something that existed independently of thought, then we would be *thinking* about that thing, so it would not exist independently of our thoughts. For example, the Kantian "thing-in-itself" is supposed to be that which exists independently of our thinking. But we are talking about it and therefore thinking about it as something that is supposedly "not thought of." In particular, we think of it as "*not* being in the domain of thought," using the human concept of negation. It could be argued that the "thing-in-itself" is that about which we are not able to say anything, but then we would have said something about it, namely that it is "indescribable." Moreover, if we cannot say anything about it, then we cannot even affirm its existence.

However, since the world only has ideas, then we cannot say that there are "only ideas" in a tone of regret. A statement is subjective only in contrast to what would be objective. But since there is no reality exterior to the mind, there is nothing objective. So we should not say that our statements are "only subjective," implying that the real world escapes us. When we think, we think about the world. The world, by being thought, exists. Because the world is made of ideas. Similarly, we must stop considering "the idea" as simply an activity of the human mind, separate from the world, an activity that would be performed "on" the world and could sometimes distort it, etc. The statement that "the world is composed of ideas" seems bizarre ("However, I do not control the world by thinking!," etc.) only to those who do not understand that ideas themselves are components of the world. If you wanted to levitate the chair in front of you and, naturally, you could not do it, this would not mean that the world is "resisting" your idea. This would not indirectly demonstrate the existence of a world outside of all thought. It would simply mean that you lack the proper idea to levitate your chair from a distance. This proper idea would be to build a machine linking your brain activity to the position of the chair via a chip, a motor, and electromagnetic waves. This machine would still be your thought, first because it would be the result of your calculations, and second, because the matter that would compose it would not have an existence independent of thought, for the reasons explained at the beginning of this solution.

So, it is because everything is "subjective" that nothing is subjective.

We finally realize that the idea and the world are consubstantial – Spinoza had intuited this through what tradition after him called the "parallelism" of Extension and Thought. Spinoza's mistake, however, was believing that Extension and Thought were incommensurable, reminding us, for example, that "the idea of a circle is not something having a circumference and a center, as a circle has, and that the idea of a body is not that body itself"[3]. Or, to use

---

[3] Spinoza, *On the Improvement of the Understanding*, §27.

Althusser's words: "The concept of a dog does not bark"[4]. But we would reply to this example: that thinking about a dog could generate the sound of barking thanks to a technology similar to the one mentioned above; that the perceived dog in front of you is no less an idea than the "just thought" dog, or that the dog thought of is no less real than the dog in front of you. Certainly, the dog in front of you and the dog "just thought" are different, but what distinguishes them is not the fact that one would belong to the Extension while the other would belong to the Thought. They are two thoughts (or two things) distinguished by the fact that: first, the first thought-thing is generally a little more vivid, orderly, clear, and stable than the second one[5]; second, these two thoughts-things are part of a network of other thoughts-things that is generally different; the first would never turn into a dragon, for example, when the second might suddenly change into a dragon through "the association of ideas" or a nightmare.

Scholium


Berkeley's main thesis was already expressed, long before him, by Nāgārjuna. In his *Treatise on the Middle Way*, this Buddhist philosopher explains that there can be no visible thing without a person who sees it. He also explains that, reciprocally, there is no vision without an object seen: if there were vision "independently of any object of vision," he writes, "it would exist before an object of vision, would be separate from this object, and would therefore see no object. How would it then be logical to say that the vision sees?"[6].

---

[4] Althusser, "Soutenance d'Amiens," in *Positions*, Paris, Éditions Sociales, 1976, p. 156.

[5] Berkeley, *Principles of human knowledge*, part I, §30.

[6] Nāgārjuna, *Treatise on the Middle Way*, Chapter III (Examination of the Senses).

## Scholium 2

We have seen that the fact of having abandoned naive realism (according to which the real world is entirely detached from ideas) does not make us "lose" anything. We are not dealing with a "smaller world." To quote Berkeley: "We are not deprived of any one thing in nature."[7]

## Scholium 3

This solution is very important because it distinguishes our purpose from Kantian antinomies. The contradiction that emerges in the solutions of this book is in the world. It is not simply our minds that are contradictory and "fail" to think about the world. We think of a world that is itself contradictory. The fact that reasoning, when rational, leads to contradiction, shows the contradiction of the world, not just the contradiction of the mind. Kant has thus shown, without realizing it, that the world is really both finite and infinite, divisible and indivisible – a point to which we shall return, since we differ from Kant in a second aspect.

---

[7] Berkeley, *Principles of human knowledge*, part I, §34.

Solution 3

There is some being; there is a "there is" that consists of thought, which is consubstantial to the thing. But there is still no particular "thought" or "thing"; there is only *some* thought or *some* world. Is there anything *in particular*?

We have seen that there is no real distinction between the act of thinking and the object of thought. And the act of thinking exists (Solution 1), therefore everything we think exists too. And it is a fact that we can indeed think about something particular. So something particular does exist. We can think, for example, of a horse. This, again, does not mean that the idea of an imaginary horse has the same characteristics as the idea of a horse we see in front of us (Solution 2).

Scholium

To be more precise, not only can we think about something in particular, but we must do so. Indeed, let's try to think only about the fact of being, in general. This means not thinking about anything in particular. Now, what has no particular determination is also nothingness. But it is impossible to think about nothingness. The reason is as follows: we have seen that there is no real distinction between the act of thinking and the object of thought. So, if the object of thinking is nothingness (*total* nothingness, not just *something* that is not), then the act of thinking is nothingness too. But that is impossible because the act of thinking always implies in itself its own existence (Solution 1).

In fact, all you have to do is try to imagine nothingness. How would we imagine it? Total darkness? In this case, there can be no shadows or contours. We cannot say *what* is dark. There are no walls, no delimited space. It is no longer even possible to *distinguish* total darkness from total brightness or anything else, which is why we actually do not imagine total darkness. In short, it is the death of all experience. Someone who thinks of nothingness cannot even know he is thinking of nothingness – otherwise, he is thinking of something, and his thought has an intended object and not nothing. Besides, thought always comes with knowledge of thought (Solution 1). So to think of nothing is to kill thought. But thought cannot annihilate itself (Solution 1). So, an entirely indeterminate thought is impossible.

Solution 4

There are things or ideas in the world – we will use these words indistinctly. But is there really a plurality of things, or is everything one?

Think of a square. Can there only be one square? A square is necessarily limited. It is a square and not something else; it is distinct from what it is not, from what is outside it, and out of its limits. Thus, the existence of the square presupposes the existence of a second thing from which it is distinguished. The same is true of every particular thing, because every particular thing, by definition, has its limits. So there is necessarily a plurality of things.

However, once two things are defined, are they really separate? Are there really two things rather than only one? We say that the first thing would have a boundary beyond which it would no longer exist. But such a boundary is shared. The boundary, at the same time, includes and excludes; it belongs to the thing that is bounded and, at the same time, indicates its end[8]. Borders are, so to speak, bridges. The bridge has two different sides, and at the same time, it connects both sides. It connects separate places. It can connect them because they are separate.

Possible objection and answer to the objection: can't we imagine two absolutely separate things? They would have no boundaries between them. For example, France and the

---

[8] Excerpt from *Écrits pour les rares personnes qui tentent d'exister,* Paris, Éditions Skhedia, 2022, p. 311-312.

Netherlands have no common border. However, France has a boundary with Belgium, which shares a border with the Netherlands. Step by step, then, France and the Netherlands do share a common area of differentiation.

So there are a plurality of things in the world that are necessarily interdependent. And, if they are all connected by bridges, can we not say that all these things form one? – in the same way that all European countries form *one* continent. But is not the division of this thing just a choice, a point of view that can be discarded? Let's take the example of land and sea. Where does the sea begin and end? Up to the sand? But should the part of the sand that is wet be included in the land or the sea? And what about the fact that some of the seawater evaporates and falls back to earth as rain? Don't we have the sea over our heads and on wet sidewalks? There is no real separation: everything is a *continuum*. Then it is no longer possible to speak of interdependence, because interdependence presupposes several things, and there is no such plurality.

But if everything is a *continuum*, then there is only one thing, namely this everything (a necessarily particular thing, see the previous solution), which is impossible because one thing necessarily implies another – see the beginning of this solution. So there are several particular things, but they are linked together in a *continuum*... and so on.

So there is only one thing, and, at the same time, there are several things.

Scholium

The same applies to the question of knowing whether only the self exists or the others also exist, although we will come back to this in more detail later. The self is different from others but thereby shares a boundary with them, and so on. The same applies to the concepts of dependence and independence. We also already have the intuition that everything is infinitely divisible and that everything can be infinitely reunited.

## Scholium 2

On the subject of the one and the many, the undivided and the divided, Leibniz thought that living beings were an exception. A bottle without a cap is still a bottle. A living being, on the other hand, has interdependent parts, so you cannot remove one part without affecting the whole. From this, Leibniz deduced that, unlike things, every organism is *one*, really indivisible, because its constituent parts are interdependent. However: a) The same applies to the bottle. Removing the cap affects its overall function: in particular, it can no longer be a container when turned upside down. b) This interdependence between the parts of an organism is limited. This is why removing one of the parts of a human body rarely destroys the human body. A human without a thumb continues to be a human, and what's more, to be the same human. No one would say that Peter, having lost his thumbs, is no longer Peter. Here, it could be argued that there are parts more essential than thumbs, the removal of which would, this time, lead to Peter's destruction – his brain or his memories, for example. But on this distinction between the essential and the superficial, see Solution 8.

## Scholium 3

The Russians are waging war on the Ukrainians. But then we can also say that the universe is at war with itself. Possible objection: if the whole universe is at war with itself when the Russians wage war on the Ukrainians, why don't the French feel this war? Answer to the objection: first of all, the French feel this war to the extent that they suffer its consequences, particularly economic ones. But we could always ask why the French are not the ones taking the bullets, which brings us to a second point: it is a question of degree of empathy. The French could very well die from these distant bullets, in the same way that a mother who loses her child can die of grief. Third, a Frenchman may have no empathy for these soldiers because it is *also* true that France is separated from Ukraine – read this solution again and, if necessary, also pay attention to the following solution on the finite and the infinite.

Solution 5

Is reality infinite? Are human beings finite?

When faced with the problem of the existence of the finite and the infinite, three answers are generally put forward: there are only finite things (a plurality, because one finite thing presupposes another, see Solution 4); there is only one infinite thing (an infinite universe); and, there are finite things included in an infinite universe.

First, we can show that the third answer is correct. In fact, we must think about the existence of a limited thing (see Solution 3). But these limits presuppose the existence of a second thing, which is necessarily linked to a third (Solution 4), and this *ad infinitum*. So, even if there were only finite things, they would have to be *infinitely* numerous – hence the possibility of always pushing back the "limits" of the universe. So there is indeed an infinity of finite things, this infinity being constructed by the infinite deployment of finite things. We understand that the world must be infinite, not "even though" there are finite things, but *by thinking* about the existence of finite things.

However, first of all, we believe that there is *one* infinite universe, so it is not infinite. Indeed, finite things form a *continuum* (Solution 4). Moreover, obviously there is only one infinite world or universe, because if we tried to think of several ones, one infinite would be limited by the others and therefore would no longer be infinite. But if there is only one, then it is not infinite. Secondly, and more importantly, this infinite would be limited from within by the finite things that constitute it, so it would not be infinite. In fact, if the infinite universe included truly finite things, it would be finitized by the finite things it includes, i.e., it would have a boundary with each finite thing. The interior of the finite thing, or its power, would *stand in front* of the infinite substance, which would thereby be limited and therefore not infinite. So we are thinking of finite things. In short, we have just shown that the first and third answers are the same: to think that there are finite things in an infinite universe is still to think that there are only finite things.

As for the attempt to think of an infinity that would be constituted neither by finite things nor by *one* infinity (we would just say: "infinity"), this amounts to thinking of the indeterminate, which is impossible (Solution 3). An infinite universe that contains nothing finite, nothing particular, we cannot think of *what* that is[9].

In conclusion: there is one finite thing, and therefore several finite things, and even an infinite number of finite things, but this is *one* infinity, and it is limited from within, that is why we think again about the existence of one finite thing, and so on.

Scholium

We are not exactly repeating the Kantian antinomies. Kant indeed points out that it is possible to demonstrate that the universe is finite, and that it is possible to demonstrate that the universe is infinite, but he does not demonstrate that the universe is finite *because* it is infinite, or that it is infinite *because* it is finite, as we have just done.

---

[9] Hence the fact that Spinoza's infinite monism is sometimes described by Hegel as acosmism – an absent world or, what is equivalent, nothingness, pure being.

# Scholium 2

By reading this solution and the previous one about the one and the many, we understand that the same applies to the ideas of parts and whole.

## Solution 6

Is everything relative?[10]

Every thing depends on everything else (see Solution 4). Therefore, every thing exists only in relation to others.

However, if everything is relative, then the statement "Everything is relative" is also relative, so the fact that everything is relative is just one point of view among others, and the other point of view, according to which everything is not relative, would also be valid. Moreover, by definition, one thing is relative *to another*. If this other thing is relative, we have to search again for what it is relative to, and if this search is repeated again, we are stuck in an infinite regress. Faced with this infinite regress, we no longer know what is the basis for the existence of the first thing that was supposed to be relative; it loses its roots. We no longer even understand how it could exist at all, so its relative nature evaporates with the thing itself[11].

The objection according to which "everything is relative except the fact that everything is relative" also leads to a contradiction. There would only be one fact in the world that would not be relative. But since everything in the world

---

[10] The order of the solutions is becoming less and less important. In some cases, a solution may suggest browsing through a subsequent solution to be fully understood. However, the essence of each solution remains comprehensible without reference to a later solution.

[11] But this does not mean that *everything* disappears because the *cogito* always makes something appear.

is interdependent (Solution 4), all it takes is one non-relative fact for all the others to also be affected by this absoluteness. For example, let's imagine that the Sun, *per impossibile*, is the only immobile thing in the universe. Then, all movements in the world could have one and only one true measurement, with the Sun as a reference.

So we see that, if everything is relative, then nothing is relative.

However, if a thing is not relative, i.e., if it is absolute, then it does not depend on any other to be. But every thing has a limit that both excludes *and includes* the other, on which, therefore, it depends.

So, if everything is relative, then everything is absolute, then everything is relative, and so on.

Solution 7

What is the truth?

Truth cannot be defined by the correspondence between idea and thing, since idea and thing are *always* consubstantial. Admittedly, we can distinguish imagination from perception, but we have seen that this distinction does not come from the fact that the former would be on the side of the subject, while the latter would be linked to the world (Solution 2).

Truth, then, must rather be a certain relationship between ideas – or between things. When this relationship is dialectical, it expresses truth. This dialectic is about bringing to light "the identity of identity and non-identity"[12], i.e., a contradiction. We conclude that truth is the rational demonstration of the irrational[13].

---

[12] Hegel, *The Difference between Fichte's and Schelling's System of Philosophy*, trans. Henry S. Harris and Walter Cerf, Albany: State University New York Press, 1977, p. 156.

[13] There's just one exception: the *cogito*. It is true without being contradictory. But, strictly speaking, it is neither contradictory nor non-contradictory, because it is neither a demonstration nor even an attempt at demonstration, but is more akin to intuition. And, to use Hegel's words, it cannot "pass into its other," because it has no other, or at least no other that would be verifiable (see scholia of Solutions 1 and 3). By the way, we say "intuition," but the truth of the *cogito* is rather uncharacterizable, because, to pass judgment *on* it, one would have to be able to grasp it from the outside of it, an outside that does not exist. Solutions 2 and the following do not

There are, moreover, all our conventional "truths"[14] that exist for practical purposes. They consist of maintaining the emphasis only on one side of the dialectical truth – and, in doing so, this truth is "de-dialectized." For example, we almost always think that land and sea are not one – probably because our human activities in these two spaces are very different, and these two ideas refer to very different networks of ideas. Conversely, we are very inclined to think that the two halves of a soccer field actually form one field, probably for a reason opposite to the one given in the previous example. The primary purpose of these conventional truths is to conceal the truth of contradiction; otherwise, we would sink into madness. Indeed, the truth of contradiction cannot and must not be fully grasped. We might compare its observation to that of lightning: it is extremely brief and must be kept at a distance. The philosopher is the one who, from time to time, pays attention to this storm that cracks the harmony of the usual construction of his existence.

## Scholium

Where we answer a possible objection.

We simplify the world by constructing dichotomous concepts – the one would not be linked in any way to the multiple, and so on. So, this simplification would only come from us and would be subjective. But we have shown that ideas are in the world. So this "subjective" process of

---

speak about the truth of the *cogito*, but they unfold the thought that has been found.

[14] What Hegel, for his part, calls a logic of the understanding. But Nāgārjuna also suggested such a distinction when he wrote, for example, "Conventionally, we can speak of 'self' or 'non-self'; but ultimately, neither 'self' nor 'non-self' exist." (*Treatise on the Middle Way*, Chapter 18, Examination of Self and Entities)

simplifying the world would still be constitutive of the world itself. So our "conventional truths" mentioned above would, in fact, be truths just as profound as the truth of contradiction.

Answer to the objection: The fact remains that there is a logic of contradiction. We can rationally demonstrate this irrationality. In our solutions, the rationality of the argument advances and, finally, in a way, sacrifices itself by jumping logically into its reverse. So, if we dig deeper into the question of whether, for example, the one is absolutely separated from the many, we will come to realize that this is not the case. The central point is the following: when we question our conventional truths, we find the truth of contradiction, whereas the converse is not true. The truth of contradiction never leads to our conventional truths – indeed, there is nothing deeper to find than the truth of contradiction. The previous objection seems to defy this "never," but in fact lacks a sequel: supposing that we were to show that our conventional, *non-contradictory* truths are no less true than the truth of contradiction, then we would arrive at a contra-diction, which would again prove the truth of contradiction.


Scholium 2


Where we answer a possible second objection.

It is true, as Aristotle demonstrated[15], that we cannot think of a contradiction – it is impossible, for example, to imagine that a cup in front of us would be completely white and completely black at the same time. But the unthinkable cannot exist (as long as the world and we exist); therefore this truth of contradiction would not exist either.

Answer to the objection: We need to make a semantic clarification here. By "contradiction," we mean the

---

[15] Aristotle, *Metaphysics*, Gamma, 4 (1005b-1009a)

perpetual alternation of thesis and antithesis, and this alternation is, for its part, thinkable[16]: we *arrive at* the antithesis by starting from the thesis, *then* find the thesis again by examining the antithesis, and so on. By the term "contradiction," we also denote this awareness that the thesis *comes from* the antithesis, and vice versa.

## Scholium 3

We might be tempted to return to the classic problem of truth-correspondence with the following remark: how can we distinguish with certainty between the idea of an imaginary horse and the idea of the perception of a horse in front of us? But this question is at the level of conventional truth since it ignores the fact that everything is a *continuum* (Solution 4) and that these two ideas are not really distinguishable. Obviously, to say that the horse in front of you is not different in nature from the imaginary horse, is surely not satisfactory to the person asking the question, even if it is true. Instead, he will need to be given a set of practical hints: "Pinch yourself, then see whether the horse disappears or not," etc. But this can only be a matter of advice, pragmatism, and probability of success.

---

[16] As we know, at the start of the *Science of Logic*, Hegel describes this alternation as "becoming": the alternation of pure being and nothingness. He sees this alternation as an "overcoming" of thesis and antithesis, a step forward: this alternation would be a new concept. This would mean that all our solutions would be incomplete, because they could go further, by thinking and going beyond the contradiction. However, to understand our difference with Hegel on this point: read the dialogue below.

Solution 8

In a being, are there, on the one hand, its essence and, on the other, its appearances?[17]

A being has many characteristics. In the case of a man, he may be short, blond, etc. A characteristic of a being is said to be only accidental when it could be changed or even removed without the being ceasing to be what it is. For example, if Peter loses his hair, we will continue to say that his name is Peter: that would be an accidental, superficial characteristic. He retains his essence.

However, referring to the solution on the one and the many, we understand that, when a given thing is modified, the things that adjoin it must also be modified. Therefore, Peter's hair loss must modify all the other parts of him. If we all say that Peter without his hair is still Peter, it is because our culture judges hair to be superficial. It is easy to imagine a culture (and very probably there is one) where what we consider superficial would be considered essential. For example, an individual who refused to receive traditional tattoos would no longer be recognized by other members of the community, even though, in our Western eyes, it is "only" ink on the "surface" of someone. To keep reducing the reader's potential astonishment at this side of the contradiction, we might add the following remarks:

---

[17] Or: the problem of distinguishing between substance and accidents; the problem of distinguishing between subject and attributes.

- What would be essential to Peter, in our culture, if not his hair? His memory, perhaps? However, for sure, Peter without any memory would still be called Peter by his loved ones – he would be recognized as Peter. Even when Peter dies, those closest to him will continue to call the lifeless body Peter. It would seem, then, that not even being alive is part of Peter's essence. If the search for essence is so difficult, it is because essence exists *and* does not exist, as we will soon understand.

- If Peter cut his hair, changed his skin color, the timbre of his voice, and the shape of his nose, four things that are apparently superficial, his friends, however, would no longer be able to recognize him. But wouldn't Peter continue to call himself Peter, even if no one else recognized him? To this objection, we have to reply, first of all, that this is indeed possible: Peter's identity could go unnoticed by everyone else, because each of us, in a way, lives in a separate world (see solution on solipsism). Secondly, this remark would only be an objection if Peter could not help but continue to recognize himself in this way. However, this is not the case; in truth, it is only a contingent decision, and, in fact, an individual can also choose to change his or her identity: for example, the writer Eddy Bellegueule (now Édouard Louis) recounts such a metamorphosis of the self.

- If Peter had a lookalike, we would say that his essence is in his thoughts, because it would be by conversing with him that we would distinguish him from the lookalike. But if two people had exactly the same personality, the same memories, and the same opinions, and one of them had the body of Peter and the other the body of James, this time we would say that the body is decisive, and therefore essential, for recognizing Peter.

All this shows that the distinction between essence and accident in a being is variable and contingent, to the point that sometimes essence and accident can be interchanged. Consequently, there really is neither essence nor accident.

But it is also true that every thing must exist and be thought of separately from everything else (Solution 4), which is why the hair exists separately from the rest of Peter, so its loss does not affect the rest of Peter, which we will call his essence. So it is reasonable to "be suspicious of appearances," since a part of a person may say nothing about that person, being in fact independent of him.

But *again, because of this separation*, Peter has no essence, and all we have in front of us is a sum of scattered things: a memory here, a body there, etc.

And so on.

Another demonstration: appearance is the appearance *of something* – for example, Peter's appearance. There is no appearance without an essence that appears. Therefore, appearance is essentially attached to essence. Indeed, it is Peter's appearance, not someone else's. We can still identify Peter by his appearance – or, to put it another way, it is indeed *his* appearance – which means that this appearance points to him, and since it points to him rather than to anyone else, this appearance is not simply "added to" Peter but is part of his essence. So it is not just appearance. Likewise, the essence must appear. If Peter never shows up, then he does not exist. His appearance is, therefore, in truth, part of his essence. Essence and appearance define each other, and each is through the other.

But, by definition, essence is not supposed to be conditioned by appearance. Peter is supposed to remain Peter, *regardless of* his appearance.

So essence, in order to be, is not. The same goes for the appearance.

## Scholium

The reader will have recognized that this topic contains the classic theme of personal identity, or the "self." Regarding the fact that the "self" is elusive, reference can be made to Hume. As to whether the "I" must be thought, we can refer to Kant, but with the added caveat that the thought of the "I" is not simply the product of the human mind but a constituent of reality (See also Solution 19).

Solution 9

Does everything pass? Here, we raise the question of time, movement, and change.

If everything passes, then it is also true that everything appears and everything stays the same. In fact, without this passage, *new* things would never appear or the present thing could not *last*. Appearance happens through disappearance, and disappearance happens through appearance. Time is, once again, a contradiction in itself: it is the disappearance of appearances, the appearance of disappearances.

Now let's go a step further to find out whether this kind of time exists at all.

First, we can demonstrate that nothing can pass. We owe this proof to Zeno of Elea. To go from 0 to 1 second, you have to pass through 0.5 seconds. To go from 0 to 0.5 seconds, you have to pass through 0.25 seconds, and so on: you'll never get any further. There is not only here an infinity to cross (the infinite divisibility of time), but we do not even cross a piece of this infinity. Indeed, with each "step" we take, we notice that we have not really been able to take that step, because we have forgotten a necessary intermediate step.

Another demonstration of the immobility of all things: suppose something goes from point A to point B, for example, an arrow. But *what* exactly is passing? This arrow? No, the arrow itself is not passing, because we keep calling it an "arrow." So, in fact, there is no passing. Or we could say that the movement "happens" to the arrow. The arrow would not move, rather there would be motion coming to the arrow. But on this subject, see Solution 8 on essence and accident.

Another demonstration of the immobility of all things: everything is interdependent (Solution 4), so if one thing were to disappear (pass away), everything would disappear into nothingness, something that is not possible (scholium of Solution 3).

But the world is not at all still. Indeed, how would we think of this immobility? We would have to check that everything is now motionless, and *then* check later that it continues to be motionless. In other words, time would continue to pass. Possible objection: time continues to pass in a world that does not pass. Time is transcendent to the world. Response to objection: This is impossible, since the world itself changes. In fact, how would we know that time is passing if we could not think of anything passing in the world? We would need to have a watch with us, but we would see the hands of that watch moving, so not everything would be still. Or we would observe this succession by using an "internal watch," a "biological watch." But, first, this would still presuppose a *change* of state within us. Second, we have seen that what happens "within us" is not irremediably separated from what happens in the world (Solution 2).

In conclusion: we have seen that nothing can pass, but for this immobility to be shown, we need the *passage* of this immobility, and *constantly*, so everything passes, but we can show that nothing can pass, and so on.

Solution 10

Does causality exist?

In the history of philosophy, the contradictory truth of causality has already been demonstrated, notably by Nāgārjuna[18] and partly by Kant.

Everything is interdependent (Solution 4), so the existence of something and its understanding can be found by referring to something from the past, called a cause.

However, since everything is interdependent, we can refer to any one thing to understand another, which contravenes the principle of causality, according to which the same effect is necessarily preceded by the same cause, which we could isolate. What's more, since everything is interdependent, we can refer to something in the future to explain something in the present, or to something in the present to explain something in the present, or to something in the present to explain something in the past, which again contravenes the principle of causality, according to which the cause temporally precedes the effect. This possibility of referring to something located anywhere in the present, past,

---

[18] Since this is the third time we have referred to Buddhism, let's have a quick look at what makes our reasoning different. Among the most important differences: according to Buddhists, everything is impermanent. But, as we have seen, it is also true that everything is permanent and immobile. According to them, everything is interdependent, but we have seen that the opposite is also true. In short, they rarely, if ever, take reasoning to its dialectical conclusion.

or future, arises from the fact that, since everything is interdependent, time does not pass.

However, if the cause is mixed with the effect in this way, we end up making the universe an indistinct whole, which must then necessarily be thought of again as *one* determinate thing, and this "emergence" of a determinate thing, "followed" by several determinate things (Solution 4), makes it possible to think of causality again, and so on. So everything is caused, and nothing is caused. Similarly, everything is causal, and nothing is causal[19]. What's more, causality can exist thanks to the absence of causality, and vice versa.

Elements of another demonstration by Nāgārjuna[20] :

"If the cause is empty of an effect[21],
How can it produce an effect?
If the cause is not empty of an effect,
How can it produce an effect, since the effect already exists?"

In summary, Nāgārjuna shows that the necessity of causality would lead to the disappearance of the temporal distinction between cause and effect (since the cause would necessarily be in the effect and vice versa), and therefore the disappearance of causality.

---

[19] Hegel would say that this corresponds to the notion of *law* in science. But is this really a step forward in thinking? On this question, read the following solution as well as the dialogue following this book.

[20] Nāgārjuna, *Treatise on the Middle Way*, Chapter 20, Examination of Combination.

[21] Which it is supposed to be, since the effect is not supposed to already be in the cause.

Nāgārjuna repeats himself here, slightly changing the terminology:

"If the effect existed in itself[22],
How could a cause produce it?
If the effect did not exist in itself,
Then, what would the cause actually produce?"

Let's take an example: the movement of the first marble causes the movement of a second marble by hitting it. If these two movements exist separately, one cannot be transmitted to the other, or passed on to the other. But if they do not exist separately, if the second movement exists thanks to the first, then it was already contained in the movement of the first marble; this first marble did not "produce" anything. Indeed, production implies the appearance of something more, something external to the first marble, but we have just assumed that the movement of the second marble did not admit of this exteriority, this separation. Finally, if only part of the movement of the second marble exists thanks to that of the first one, the problem still arises, at least for this part: was this part "produced" by a cause, or was it already in the cause? Neither the thesis nor the antithesis are tenable. This part must have been in the cause, so that we can speak of cause and transmission, and, at the same time, it must be elsewhere than in the cause, to continue speaking of something causing and something caused. The same reasoning applies to the origin of a part of this part, and so on.

---

[22] That is, if it had an absolute existence, distinct from the cause.

## Scholium

Aristotle tries to solve this problem using the notion of the possible. The first marble would contain the movement of the second, but only *potentially*. However, first, we would have to explain this transition from possibility to action, and on this point, see the solution on time. Secondly, we could ask ourselves where this possible comes from, that is to say, what is its cause, and to do so, we would have to resort to another possible, *ad infinitum*, in such a way that we would never know exactly how the possible in the first marble can be.

Solution 11

Do 1 and 1 make 2?

This problem can be solved by referring to Solution 4, about the one and the many.

$1 + 1 = 2$ only if $2 = 1 + 1$, i.e., if 2 is divisible into two (equal) parts. In fact, this is possible. One thing necessarily implies a second thing (Solution 4), so 2 indeed comes from 1.

However, precisely because 2 comes from 1, it is, in some sense, still 1. We can see 2 as *a* thing, a *continuum* (Solution 4). So, there is always only one thing, and we will never get to two. Or we could write $2 = 1$, which mathematics refuses to do.

We could also point out that 2 necessarily implies a third thing, which necessarily implies a fourth, etc., leading us to think that $2 = 3 = 4...$ an indistinction that makes mathematics impossible.

However, from this indistinct whole, we return to two particular things during a brief "instant" of thought (Solution 4), and so on. Mathematics chooses to "pause" at this moment. In short, they eliminate and simplify the truth of the contradiction (see Solution 7).

So 1 and 1 make 2, and they do not make 2.


Scholium

Where we answer a possible objection.

Instinctively, we might believe that we can resolve the contradiction as follows: we see two trees in front of us; there are indeed *two* trees because they are slightly different, and there are indeed two *trees*, two beings grouped into *one category*[23]. The idea here is that their identity would be essential and their differences superficial: these trees would have more similarities than differences, but enough differences to be two – or the other way around, it does not matter. Readers will come back to Solution 8 to see that the contradiction remains.

Scholium 2

This contradiction does not just invalidate mathematics, because mathematics also works *thanks to* contradictions.

In fact, let's consider this equality again: $1 + 1 = 2$. On the one hand, this statement posits a 1 and *another* 1. On the other hand, the first 1 cannot be different from the second, because mathematics says that $1 = 1$. My right thumb, and my right thumb again, still makes my right thumb. $1 + 1 = 1$.

Let's say it again: in the statement "$1 + 1 = 2$," there is 1, then another 1, and yet it is not the same 1. Otherwise, we stand still and never get to 2. There is the addition of a new 1 and, at the same time, there is only the repetition of the same 1. Two things are one and two at the same time, which is what we were talking about in Solution 4. Mathematicians are unaware that mathematics contains this contradiction.

---

[23] On this question, Nietzsche's *Human, All Too Human*, I, §19, may prove useful. See also fragments 141 and 150 collected by A. Kremer-Marietti in *Le livre du philosophe*, Paris, GF, 1991. However, the perceptive reader will notice that Nietzsche justifies only one side of the contradiction here, arguing that differences are somehow essential, without seeing that identity is also essential.

Their famous principle of non-contradiction includes contradictions, and their famous tautology includes differences.

The remarkable thing about mathematics is that a huge theoretical edifice is built (and therefore stable) from a contradiction (and therefore unstable), and that this edifice also has many useful implications for our everyday lives, making it *like a* bridge between conventional truth and the truth of contradiction[24]. Physics, unlike mathematics, has been entangled for centuries in the false framework of naïve realism, which for a long time prevented it from having the same depth as mathematics, until the advent of quantum physics – where contradiction is sometimes accepted, where the dichotomy between subject and object comes to an end, and where physics, unsurprisingly, becomes very much mathematized.

---

[24] They are like a bridge because of the following double fact: they are driven by contradiction, but at the same time, mathematicians must not think about this contradiction, they must act *as if* it did not exist, otherwise, they would be "standing still" and risking the madness mentioned above. This, again, is remarkable.
In this regard, let's take the example of the mathematized *law* of gravity. Does the Moon attract the Earth, or is it the other way around? Both. But that's unthinkable. We always think one or the other, or, at the very least, one and *then* the other. We could speed up this alternation in our minds, but never manage to think both at the same time: It would be like managing to think that this dog is all black and all white at the same time. *But* we have Newton's equation: mathematics can approach this unthinkable. However, we must insist on the word "approach." As Feynman famously said, "Nobody really understands quantum mechanics," but quantum mechanics fits into equations. We can mathematize the idea that a particle is there and not there at the same time. But let's not claim that mathematics allows us to think about this fact. Mathematics acts *as if* it were not a problem, just as we can decide to simply write or say: "I am and I am not."

Solution 12

Am I the only one who thinks? In other words, are there other consciousnesses besides mine, or are "others" merely objects of my thought? We recognize here the problem of solipsism.

This problem only exists if we think that, in Solution 1, a thinking "I" was present. However, we have never demonstrated this. There was no thinking "I," we just noticed that there was *some* thought[25]. Then we noticed that the world and thought were consubstantial. So, *everything* thinks. I think, the world thinks, even the rock thinks[26] – an intuition that Spinoza had when he wrote that every event in the Extension corresponds to an event in Thought. So it is true that others think too. The world thinks and all *parts* of the world think too (see Solution 4), so it is also true that my thought is separate from that of others, just as it is true that this separate thought must be a thought.

---

[25] Husserl has remarked that Descartes went too far when he asserted, without proof, that the *cogito* expresses an "I" who thinks. This is an opportunity for us to point out that, in Solution 1, strictly speaking, we should have written that there is *cogitatio*. We have obviously kept the term *cogito* for reasons of tradition.

[26] But what does such an "inanimate entity" think? Science can tell us. For example, the Sun is governed by physico-chemical laws that belong to it, i.e., that are not simply projected onto it by the human mind.

We could also write that the world and its parts, including others, are "composed of" thought[27]. And regarding terminology again: the fact that "the rock thinks" seems odd only if we consider that thought is necessarily a powerful action. But, in truth, thinking is not enough to bring about powerful action. Let's recap: we can say that "the rock is composed of thought" – just like anything else. And it is also true that "it thinks," that thought is its action, because everything is both active and passive, free and determined (see next solution). But the action of the rock is so weak when the action of man can be so strong (as Spinoza shows in the *Ethics*), that we understand the tendency to say that it is false that "the rock thinks."

Another demonstration: there is thought (Solution 1). Let's assume that this thought comes from an "I," which would be part of the world. But there is nothing "in" a thing that does not extend to others (Solution 4). So everything thinks, including other people. And, as parts, these men are quite different.

## Scholium

Here, we could not prove that nothing thinks: see Solution 1.

## Scholium 2

As for the question of the origin of thought, it is unsolvable. Indeed, we could always ask the question of the origin of this origin, and so on. What also makes this question

---

[27]Here we ask ourselves the question of whether we *are* thought or whether we produce the thought. If we produce it, we could say that we *have* it. The reading of this solution can therefore be completed with that of Solution 18 on being and having.

unsolvable is that the origin of thought would still be thought. Here, we have to look for an unthought moment, an absence of thought that would produce thought. But we have seen that such nothingness is impossible or unverifiable[28]. The same applies to the origin of the world, as thought and the world are consubstantial. What we can assert is that everything thinks and that each part thinks separately, so in a way, each part possesses its own thought, but these possessors are themselves composed of thought.

Scholium 3

We see that it is false that "thought comes from the brain," for the same reasons as in the previous scholium. We could ask the question of the origin of the brain, and so on. What is more, it is generally accepted that the brain is matter, understood as something absolutely not made up of thought and yet existing, which is impossible.

Of course, when a man's brain ceases to function, he is said to cease thinking[29]. However, this error of judgment is the result of a previous error, which consisted in asserting, when he was alive, that his thought was only his own and within him – read again the solution on the one and the many, as well as the solution we are dealing with here. In

---

[28] Just as it is not possible to verify (or refute) the idea that our whole world is the product of a computer simulation. Indeed, even if we were to find this computer producing this simulation, we could always be told that the perception of this computer is itself the product of a computer simulation, and so on. Similarly, the "whole" thought-world could "ultimately" take as its origin and container a vase, or an apricot, or anything else: all these hypotheses are unverifiable and irrefutable.

[29] And it is true that neuroscience brings to light a determinism (the fact that ideas of neural connections determine certain ideas of a human being) but, by this very fact, we can free ourselves (see next solution).

truth, when a man dies, his thought loses much in activity, but it does not cease to be (it becomes a legacy), and, from a certain point of view, nothing passes (Solution 9).

As for the question of whether a person who dies could leave thought (or the world), see the first scholium of Solution 1.

Solution 13

Can man act freely or is he determined by what surrounds him?

According to Spinoza, man is not free because what he believes to be his "choice" is in fact determined[30] by an infinite number of prior events, most of which are beyond his control – for example, a child's personality depends largely on the way he is brought up by his parents. What is more, man is only a tiny part of the universe, so he would be very much like crushed by it – what is called human finitude.

This book is coming to an end, as we note that this question could be resolved not only by letting the reader follow the method to which he is now accustomed, but also by inviting him to reread the solutions on causality, on the infinite and the finite, on the one and the many. Regarding this last solution, for example, we will reason as follows: someone is said to be determined by something else when that something has power over him, and this power neither comes from him nor is understood by him. However, we can also show that this power comes from him since everything is a *continuum* and he is, therefore, that "other" thing. So this thing determines him from within, and such internal necessity corresponds to freedom, as explained in Spinoza's *Ethics*[31]. In

---

[30] "Being determined" is understood here as "being caused," not as possessing a particular trait.
[31] Spinoza did not grasp the full dialectic of freedom, for one of the blind spots of Spinozism is the work of distinguishing between interior and exterior.

other words, determinism assumes that a part, such as a human being, would be *just* a part, clearly separated from the whole. However, we have shown that the opposite is also true (cf. Solution 4), and indeed, Spinoza has some intuition about this when he understands that the part is *some* whole, is made of that whole from which it derives its own activity or freedom – because the whole, encountering nothing external (by definition), is perfectly active and self-determining.

Here we can make a further point about the acquisition of this control or freedom. When we understand a cause that determines us, we know at the same time how to distance ourselves from that cause (if it weakens us) or how to redirect it in our favor. For example, it is by studying a virus that medical or computer scientists hope to finally find an antivirus. They know that knowledge enables action[32]. However, we could argue that these researchers are *determined* to find the antivirus or not (loss of control). However, they may *know* the determinism of this search (new gain of control). However, the latter knowledge is itself determined, and so on.

Scholium

Where we answer a possible objection.

Possible objection: suppose teachers are teaching a student they know is socially determined to fail academically. From their external point of view, they say and know clearly that he is determined. Now, this clear knowledge must necessarily lead to the student's liberation. However, the student is unaware of his determinisms, so he does not free

---

[32] To learn more about how such control can be acquired, we cannot recommend highly enough the reading of the *Ethics*.

himself from them. In conclusion, the student would end up both liberated and not liberated[33].

Response to the objection: first of all, if teachers clearly know that this student is adversely determined, they will necessarily know how to liberate him from the analyzed determinism, and generally it will consist of making him aware of this determinism. So the problem evaporates because the student will also be liberated from his point of view. But it is also possible that the teachers liberate him without him knowing, which revives the problem and leads us to the second part of the answer.

Second, absolutely speaking, it is true that each thing is free *and* determined, as we have just seen. In fact, we could say that teachers are determined to have this knowledge about the student's determinism, among other things. We could also say that the student, if completely unaware of his determinism, is really not determined[34]. This is not so surprising: Sure he will not go on to higher education, but that is a weakness only in the eyes of the teachers. Here we note that what Spinoza calls an increase and decrease in power are not (or rather not only) objective data, but are always apprehended within a certain network of values, a certain meaning given by the interested party to his existence – as Nietzsche has taught us. In this case, depending on the meaning the student gives to his existence (see Solution 14 on meaning), this

---

[33] And this contradiction is indeed a problem here, because it appears in a conventional, practical framework. What will the teacher *see*? What will happen to the student? Will the events of the universe split into two different courses?

[34] In the same way, an individual living in a "totalitarian" regime (but for him, it is not), seduced by its "propaganda" (but for him, it is not) and unaware of the nature of other possible regimes, would really, from his point of view, be a citizen of a free state. As for the fact that, in a certain sense, everyone lives in "his own world," see Solution 12 on solipsism and Solution 6 on relativity.

student may well be delighted not to go on to higher education – and it is not impossible to imagine a scenario where this increase of power "for him" ends up generating a clear and remarkable increase of power in the eyes of everyone because, after all, teachers, like all other human beings, are unaware of a great many causes that may invalidate their analysis of what may or may not liberate this student. Finally, it should be pointed out that the choice to pay attention to certain causes and not others is always made according to a certain starting hypothesis, according to certain prioritized criteria, and, therefore, according to a certain meaning given to existence.

Scholium 2

On the finitude of man and the possibility of showing the opposite statement (an "infinitude"), see the solution on the one and the many, and the solution on the finite and the infinite. Let us just say here that man thinks of himself as finite insofar as he is simply a part of a whole, but we have seen that there is also only one *continuum* – and, from the point of view of personal experience, it is perhaps possible for someone to briefly feel this contradiction, namely that he is the world, and this in a way that would not be madness, as some mystics try to do[35]. Let us remember one last time that we have not simply shown that man is both a part of a whole and this whole, but also, and more importantly, that he can only be a part of a whole by being this whole, for the part presupposes the whole and vice versa. In other terms, it is not

---

[35] See in particular the concept of "oceanic feeling". However, we do not show that it would be preferable (in practice) to experience this feeling rather than a sense of finitude. This is not an object of demonstration.

only the finite that depends on the world containing it, but also the world that depends on the activity of the finite.

As for the somewhat provocative objection that a personal misfortune such as being attacked by a tiger would certainly remind us of our finitude, we reply first of all that it has been proven that man is finite, separate from other finite things and their power. Second, in the face of such an attack, what makes this individual feel his finitude is above all the risk of death, which would be understood by him as a cessation of thought. But nothing can be shown about such a "cessation" (scholium of Solution 1), so nothing can be shown about the human relationship to this "cessation" either – anything is possible, and indeed, the relationship to death varies greatly from culture to culture and from era to era, and is not always based on anguish or a "cessation of world-thought." As is already well known, death is generally seen as another stage in life – so, in a way, death would not exist. For example, among Hindus, funerals are more ceremonies of passage than of mourning. Or most soldiers see the sacrifice of death, when it seems necessary, as an action – and this precisely because the soldier's awareness of being a whole (the "motherland") is very strong: so he thinks, in a way, that he is not dying but rather becoming "immortal for the motherland." As for the judgment that, in these two examples, the anguish linked to death would simply be hidden or repressed, this is excessive and would require reading Solution 14 on meaning. Finally, as to the fact that everyone would at least avoid pain and that this would be proof of "objective finitude", any psychologist with a minimum of qualification knows that, on the contrary, people often seek pain – we can also read Nietzsche on this subject.

Generally speaking, the reaction of astonishment at the truth of contradiction is to be expected when we try to relate it to practical life, which is almost always structured by conventional truths. We try to dispel this astonishment mostly in cases where we consider it likely to arise when confronted with even a single side of the contradiction. For example, the idea that man is only a part of the universe astonishes almost nobody, whereas the idea that there is only one *continuum* astonishes almost everybody, for both cultural and pragmatic reasons.

Scholium 3

Since we have just criticized the idea of a constant avoidance of pain, it may also be appropriate here to mention Spinoza's *conatus* principle, according to which "Each thing, in so far as it is in itself, endeavors to persist in its own being." (*Ethics*, III, 6).

From a survival point of view, this principle is far from always true. Some humans sacrifice themselves for others. Biologists often observe that an individual can sacrifice himself for other genetically related individuals (kin selection). Spinoza understands the possibility of one *conatus* allying itself with another, but he never goes so far as to think that they are one – on the problem of finite modes yet immersed in a single infinite substance, see Solution 5. This reminds us once again of the *continuum* from the one to the many. As we go from one thing to the next, noticing that each thing tends to persevere in its being *also* means that the whole tends to persevere in its being – and this is true because we have seen that the world-thought cannot annihilate itself (Solution 1).

Scholium 4

We mentioned the idea of some men being "freer" than others, just as we said earlier that a rock would be "less" active than a man. This is, therefore, a good opportunity to examine the question of *degree*. The degree is a certain quantity, and the quantity is a certain number, so here we must refer to Solution 11 on mathematics. From this, we will deduce that the degree, like the number, exists and does not exist. Moreover, to say that the Pacific Ocean is "bigger" than the Indian Ocean is both true and not true, since their boundaries are arbitrary, at least on one side of the contradiction (see Solution 4). But when it comes to freedom, it is harder to understand. Indeed, how can we understand that, according to one side of the contradiction, the universe would not be more active than man? or that a man would not be more active than a chimpanzee? The obstacles to this understanding are still cultural; more precisely, they relate to the general sense of existence and the world in our everyday culture. On further reflection, we would accept that it is not totally absurd for some people to give objects a high level of thought activity – and we were situated in our cultural axiology when we said that the rock is, in a way, a "small thought." We might also note that, in earlier centuries, we attributed far less active thought to animals. In the same way, we understand that the statement that "the bee has a less active thought than man" depends, in fact, on a debatable definition of intelligence, linked to a certain meaning that could be different. For example, if we believed that the higher the density of neurons in an animal, the more intelligent it is, then the bee would be more intelligent than man.

Solution 14

Does the world make sense?

The world does make sense. In fact, it is enough to make sense of the world for it to make sense. There are two reasons for this: first, thought is consubstantial with the world, so the meaning that is thought about the world is not expressed "on" the world, nor is it condemned to remain "only the meaning of a thought." Second, man has a control through which he can make this meaning occur (see solution on freedom), i.e., he can manage to encounter confirmations of this meaning in a non-imaginary mode (on the distinction between imagination and perception, see Solution 2).

However, in this project, he may not be able to achieve this meaning, because he is determined (see solution on freedom), which may lead him to lose hope and, ultimately, give up on this meaning. What is more, he could just as easily choose another meaning. If he becomes aware of this contingency, he will probably be disappointed. Because the possession of a "meaning of the world" traditionally presupposes the exclusion of this contingency of meaning: it would be the only correct meaning[36]. In other words, this meaning would be objective, and the world would retain this meaning even without any thinking being in the world – which is impossible, because the world and thought are consubstantial. So we have killed the meaning by showing that, from a certain point of view, it is "anthropomorphic."

---

[36] "The unique Number that cannot be another..." (Mallarmé)

No meaning is absolute or sacred, no meaning is "the right meaning," and this kills meaning: to be able to attribute *any* meaning to the world shows that the world has no meaning.

However, to the thought of meaning, man can add the thought that he has not simply chosen this thought[37], and then it becomes truly "non-subjective"[38].

However, from an observer's point of view, this second thought is itself the object of a choice, and so on.

So the world both makes sense and does not make sense.

## Scholium

Since God is understood as the expression of a (more or less hidden) meaning of the world, this solution also answers the question of God's existence.

## Scholium 2

"The world makes sense and it does not make sense": this is obviously a contradiction. But a contradiction is generally understood as nonsense. Thus, according to this terminology, the world and existence are indeed, in depth, driven by nonsense. However, this does not mean that the

---

[37] This is what Spinoza shows in the appendix to the first part of the *Ethics*: men attribute human traits to God (and to the course of things in general) and then worship this God, which presupposes that they have forgotten the human origin of the divine characteristics. Feuerbach refers to this more explicitly in *The Essence of Christianity*.

[38] And this is what neither Spinoza nor Feuerbach see, unlike Nietzsche, who understands that everything is interpretation, and therefore that interpretations are not *just* interpretations. On this subject, see the first scholium of solution 13.

world cannot have meaning, but rather that the very fact that meaning can be attributed to it, is part of its fundamental nonsense. In this regard, it may be worth rereading the first scholium of Solution 7 on truth.

57

Solution 15

Do good and evil exist? Are they objective or subjective?

To follow the values of good and evil is to see meaning in one's existence and the world, whether that meaning is already there or it is possible to bring it about. Accomplishing or understanding this meaning is good. Not fulfilling it or not knowing it is evil. So here we will refer to Solution 14 on meaning.

Solution 16

In morals, should we adopt a deontologism or a self-centered kind of consequentialism?

Suppose a labor reform is about to be passed in a country, and the majority of workers are opposed to it. However, there are 30% strikers on the first day of the strike, and it is announced that this figure will most probably not be exceeded on the second. So, in a way, going on strike is in vain, as the government will not back down against a minority. Among the first strikers, a deontologist will go on strike again "as a matter of principle." Kant showed that this is because this individual has a certain relationship with the universal: he tells himself that, if *all* opponents went on strike (like him), then the reform would not pass. In other words, he obeys a whole, even though this whole remains imaginary – that is, even though this whole will never be realized. The egoistic consequentialist, even if opposed to the reform, will calculate that it is not worth losing a second day's pay by going on strike, because there will not be enough strikers to win. In other words, this individual sees himself first and foremost as *part* of a whole. The individual prevails over the whole. Or, at least, the whole is only the sum of its parts.

To solve this problem, we must therefore refer to Solution 4 on the one and the many. The reader will understand that, so to speak, the deontologist is not sufficiently aware that he is also only a part of the whole, that he will therefore always be separate from the whole and that his ambition is somewhat utopian. The egoistic consequentialist, on the other hand, is not sufficiently aware that he is a part *of the whole* and that his egoism will therefore very quickly turn against him. Alternatively, a rational egoist would take greater account, in his calculations, of the long-term effects of the whole on the part, but then he would no longer simply be an egoist[39].

---

[39] Some philosophers see that you have to be altruistic to be rationally egoistic, and egoistic to be efficiently altruistic. The Spinozist theory of rational egoism and Benthamian utilitarianism can be explored in this respect. However, the reader will notice that these theories do not quite manage to hold the contradiction in practical life (which is impossible), but skillfully go back and forth between the two sides of the contradiction, which is obviously still very valuable.

Solution 17

What is the relationship between body and mind? Are they one thing, are they linked, or are they very clearly separate?

To begin with, let us recall that we have shown that the body cannot be something material – understood as existing independently of all thought (see Solution 2). What is more, we have shown that it is even more false that thought would come from such a matter (see Scholium 3 of Solution 12). This reminds us that body and mind must be two consubstantial ideas (or things), like all other ideas, which makes us see the unity of body and mind in the first place. In fact, it is because body and mind are two ideas that psycho-somatics is possible: it shows the interdependence of body and mind, and, therefore, in a way (see Solution 4 on the one and the many), it shows that they are *one*.

However, still referring to Solution 4, we understand that body and mind, like all things, are separate. We again realize that it is *because* our bodies and minds are inter-dependent that they are not: the interdependence of *two* things presupposes a strong connection and, at the same time, a clear separation, since we grasp, within the very concept of interdependence, a necessary plurality.

Scholium

Regardless of whether body and mind are one thing or separate, we can ask ourselves if we *are* or *have* this thing or these things. On this subject, see Solution 18 on being and having.

Scholium 2

Few readers will likely be surprised that body and mind are separate, whereas many are likely to be surprised that the reverse is also true. We anticipate their reaction: "How can my body and mind be one and the same thing? I can see my body outside of me, whereas my mind is inside me, so they're clearly different. Worse yet, my body and mind would be one with the rest of the world, including other bodies and other minds, so I would not really have a body and mind *of my own*?" It is therefore appropriate that we add a few words about this side of the contradiction.

It is true that the interdependence of the idea of "our body" and the idea of "our mind" or the self is very strong. However, we might note that:

- For some "mentally ill" people, attacking an "external" object that is important to them feels exactly like an attack on their body. Even "normal" people can think that a foreign body is their own: these are the proprioceptive drifts (or body transfer illusions) that psychology studies.[40]

- More commonly, damaging one's possessions often damages one's body (depression, suicide...) and vice versa – in the case of serious illness, there is no time to take care of one's possessions;

---

[40] The most famous illusion is that of the rubber hand (Botvinick & Cohen, 1998). The subjects' left hand is taken out of their sight. Instead, they see a left hand made of rubber. If the real and fake left hands are stroked simultaneously and in the same direction, the subjects begin to feel the rubber hand as if it were their own. When asked to indicate where their left hand is with their right, they very often point to the rubber hand.

- The experience of empathy shows the extent to which degrading the body or mind of a loved one can degrade the body or mind of the one who loves;

- Technological advances can make our bodies external: writing as exosomatic memory, prostheses, brain chips, and so on, are blurring the boundary between inside and outside, to the point where we can even think of this boundary disappearing.

This shows that our body is also dependent on the outside world and, therefore, not just "ours." In our culture, we generally regard the mind as sharable (through dialogue, conformism, advertising, and hypnotic influence, among others) when the body would not be so – and both are true (on one side of the contradiction) because each thing is linked to everything and each thing is separate from everything. However, if our body is strongly linked to our mind and our mind is sharable, then it must be deduced that our body is also sharable – a hypnotist can move "our" body, as can a boss, an advertiser, or a musician. Likewise, an individual or collective influencer can lead people to lose or gain weight in a particular area of their body, and so on. So, starting from the fact that our mind and body are interdependent, we have clearly noticed:

- That they form a *continuum* of things-thoughts and therefore are *also* a single thing and are, therefore, not interdependent because this would presuppose plurality;

- That they form a *continuum* of things-thoughts with "other" bodies and minds, and, therefore, do not constitute an impregnable inner fortress – although they are that *too*, which supports everyday practice in our culture that sometimes insists on this side of the contradiction even about the mind.

As for the idea that our mind would be *more* connected to our body than to other bodies, we should first refer to the scholium on quantity (Scholium 4 of Solution 13). Second, it should be pointed out that this is a (biological) determinism from which it would then be possible to free ourselves (Solution 13), notably through future biotechnologies radically transforming or extending the body, or transferring a "self" from one body to another.

Solution 18

What is the relationship between being and having?

The point here is simply to show how, to resolve this question, we need to refer to Solution 8 on the essential and the accidental. The link is as follows: what we have corresponds to something we can get rid of without ceasing to be ourselves. What you have can be put in front of you – so it would not reach you, just like an accident. On rereading this solution, the reader will understand that the opposite can also be shown. Reference should also be made to Scholium 2 of Solution 17 when we note that what a man possesses may not, in fact, be external to him – this man then being, in a way, possessed by his possession.

If we condense the argument: a man who possesses something can be said to *be* a *possessor*. In other words, this possession characterizes the man's being. If the thing possessed exists independently of the possessor, then it resists the possessor, it is not entirely in his service. The more it is at his service, the more he is its possessor. But the more he is its possessor, the more it merges with him, and from then on, he no longer possesses anything, i.e., we would say, for example, that there is a robot-man, rather than a man who possesses a robot.[41]

---

[41] Hegel makes a similar point in his famous dialectic of domination and servitude (*Phenomenology of Spirit*), explaining that the more the master owns the slave, the more he himself is a slave.

Solution 19

Am I still the same as time goes by?

The whole world does not pass, so neither do I (see solution on time).

The whole world passes and so do I (see solution on time), that is, each of my personality traits passes away.

As for the attempt to divide, on the one hand, a self that would last through time and, on the other, attributes of that self that would pass, see solution on the essential and the accidental.

Solution 20

Where we show how previous solutions can now be used to understand the contradiction of new statements, using two trivial examples:

- A man eats an apple and does not eat it;

- Day and night are one and the same thing. These statements can be demonstrated by referring to the solutions about the one and the many, about time and causality. In fact, a man cannot eat an apple because he is indistinguishable from the apple, and because nothing disappears in the world – but the opposite can also be demonstrated and thus supports practical experience. Or, day and night are one and the same thing because time does not pass, so "day" is already there (or still there) when it is dark – but the opposite can also be proven and therefore supports practical experience[42].

---

[42] This is a good opportunity to point out that the work of the sophists of antiquity, who set out to demonstrate everything and its opposite, was philosophical. However, they were sometimes unaware of this, saw their knowledge as a means of acquiring power and wealth by deceiving, or believing they were deceiving, and their demonstrations were often far less rigorous than those of, say, Hegel or Heraclitus.

Final scholia

1.

If we combine all these solutions, we notice that the truth of the contradiction tends towards the unthinkable – so towards nothingness[43]. One would have to think, for example, that an individual is free while being determined while being free while being determined... So, whoever ends up throwing away this book will more or less have understood it. For practical reasons, readers also generally have to forget this book.

2.

Sometimes the truth of the contradiction influences, so to speak, practical life. For example, we can observe the weakness of a love in which the partners would like to be independent, as well as the weakness of a love in which the partners would like to merge. Or again, it would be bad for a body to always be at rest, just as it would be bad for it to always be physically active, always moving. It has to be said that this is quite remarkable – without being entirely

---

[43] But without becoming a fallacy. This is comparable to the entirely counter-intuitive yet clearly proven fact that a particle can be in a superposition of two different states, according to the Copenhagen interpretation of quantum physics.

surprising since lovers and bodies are real, and reality is contradictory.

However, we also quickly grasp the limits of this observation, i.e., the impossibility of deducing practical advice from the truth of contradiction. Indeed, it would make no sense to advise people to be one and two with their love partner, or to be completely still and completely in motion – and that totally and partly, and so on. What is more, the contradictions contradict each other, since, for example, those who wish to be one with their partner could argue that this is what gives meaning to their lives and that all meanings are defensible and so on. In short, the more we try to see the truth of contradiction in practical life, the more we fail to do so, because the more we head towards something unthinkable or madness that will hinder practical life. Although not entirely comparable, most philosophers and scientific researchers feel the same way when they conclude that, the more they know, the less they know.

What helps in practical life is to handle the logic of understanding, that is, to consider only one side of the contradiction, or even better: to skillfully go back and forth from one side to the other, as scientists or, for example, Spinoza do.

3.

Beyond the truth of contradiction, there are: conventional truths, pragmatism, playing and, finally, the experience of art.

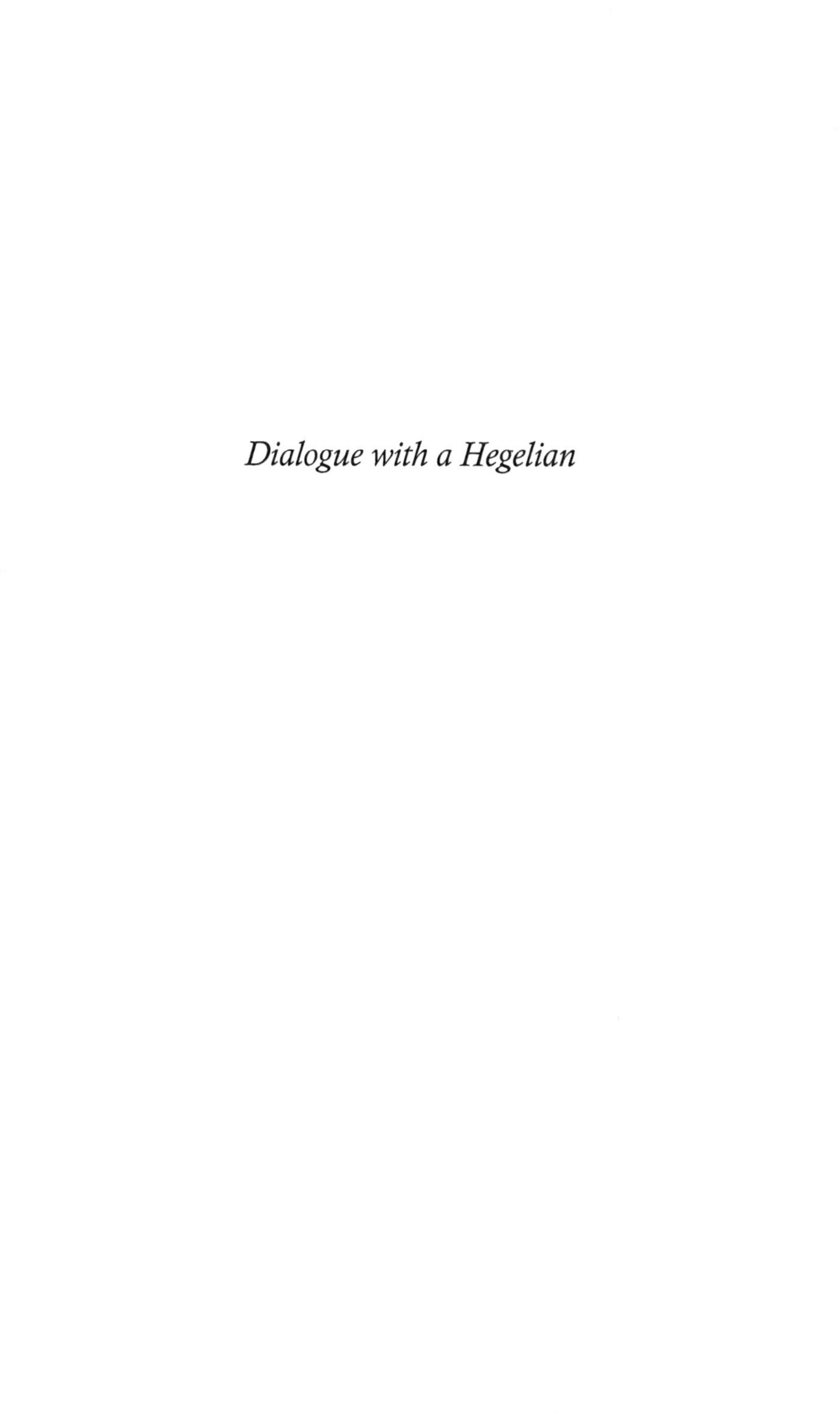

*Dialogue with a Hegelian*

Foreword

This dialogue took place in May 2021, almost two years before the writing of *Brief Solutions*. Its starting point was my reaction to a video by Loïc Maréchalen[44] on the subject of freedom and determinism according to Hegel. The reader will note that several of the ideas I am expressing below differ from those I wrote two years later. Obviously, in my view, one should agree only with those contained in *Brief Solutions*. However, reading this dialogue has two benefits. First, it gives an idea of the origin of this book – origin and not foundation, so the reading of what follows should not condition the reading of what precedes. Second, and more importantly, it highlights the similarities and differences between the Hegelian method and the one we have used so far.

L. F.

---

[44] Loïc Maréchalen has created the YouTube channel *La chose en soi*, which deals with Hegelian dialectics: his simple but never simplistic approach is an excellent introduction to Hegel.

First message

*From Léonor Franc to Loïc Maréchalen*

Thank you for this very dense and clear work.

Thanks to your examples and expressions, neophytes have a chance of understanding Hegel, and, thanks to how precisely you explain concepts, people more accustomed to philosophy will also find something to their liking. I do not know to what extent you personally subscribe to your presentation of Hegel. But since we often speak very well of what we believe to be true, I am going to assume that you consider this presentation to be entirely true. In that case, I will take the liberty of sharing with you what, in my opinion, remains problematic or insufficient in the defended position.

My comments will mostly raise questions – which you will not be required to answer, I am simply submitting them for your consideration. Furthermore, this is not a call to throw Spinoza or Hegel into the fire, since they remain, in my opinion, among the four or five greatest philosophers. My observations will be in no particular order, a little out of laziness, and also because I do not really believe in systems (sorry), but only perhaps in man's irresistible urge to systematize.

You say: "Proponents of this 'absolute' determinism advise us to combat any naive sense of illusory freedom. Let us note that they themselves fall into this naivety, since such advice is totally useless if we have no choice but to accept or reject it. This is a well-known remark, which is often used against this theory."

In fact, but as I am sure you know, this objection, known as the lazy argument, is very old, and determinist thinkers have tried to refute it. There is the refutation of some Stoics that does not seem as convincing to me as Spinoza's: he understands that he himself is determined to criticize the illusion of free will, but this criticism increases his power of action, and that is all he is interested in: not to pretend to no longer be determined, but to be determined by his nature as a man rather than by the venom of a snake. And where does this "will" to be determined by one's own nature come from? It is not a choice: it is in the nature of every thing to strive to be determined by its own nature (= *conatus*). It is human nature to want to find a vaccine against a virus, and so on. And why this *conatus*, this power of self-affirmation? Because every thing is part of what is the most self-positing, namely God or Nature. You cannot trace it back beyond that. God is somehow without reason. There is a "there is" for no reason. But now I am getting out of Spinozism. To answer your question in a nutshell – "such an invitation is totally useless if one does not have the choice, neither to accept it, nor to refuse it": such an invitation is totally useful because, precisely, Spinoza's invitation *being true, we cannot not accept it*. Our human nature, wanting to posit itself, cannot reject this truth. In any case, this is Spinoza's project. Truth would be a binding power.

You also say, "The world is both totally determined and totally free." Yes, and that is what a determinist, namely Spinoza, says. The world is totally self-determined (= free) when considered as a whole, *but* each part of the world is totally determined by something other than itself. See Spinoza's difference (which, however, brings many more questions than answers) between Naturing Nature and

Natured Nature. All this to say that I think it is a mistake to conclude that "freedom and determinism are one and the same": they are one and the same only in the case of Naturing Nature = the Whole = God. You must not mix the point of view of the Whole with that of the part. However, I understand that you have mainly tried to criticize the least subtle versions of determinism, let us say the determinism of most scientists. Tackling Hegel via Spinoza would have taken a long time.

About consciousness being freedom in Hegel: we would then have to confront scientific experiments that are able to predict states of consciousness. There is nothing easier nowadays than forcing a consciousness to think about something, the compelling consciousness most likely being compelled to compel, by another consciousness or group of consciousnesses, and so on.

You say: "Thought, because of the perspective it adopts on the mechanism, in a strict sense it interrupts the causal chain." A mechanist would say that it is always a question of a mechanism that takes a step back on itself... That is to say that this step back is a mechanical gesture... So it is not really a step back.

However, you may notice that I am slipping into a confirmation bias: we can *always* pretend we are dealing with a new mechanism. If we cannot see it, we will say: there are hidden variables, and one day we will understand that it is all mechanical! That is what Einstein thought about quantum mechanics: *for now*, we would just *believe* that it is indeterministic. Even today, one can defend Einstein, because despite the refutation of the principle of locality he believed in, there could still be determinism strangely without the principle of locality – but I do not know this field very well.

Similarly, we could at least suppose that we are *externally* determined to "internalize determinism." It sounds like you might be taking this into account when you write: "Freedom is only determinism that (through consciousness) refines itself [so far, I would agree] to enable the emergence, in itself, of an open rather than closed causality." And here is *the* thing that deserves further explanation, namely the distinction between open and closed causality. Is it Hegelian? Is open causality a "soft" causality? a causality in which everything is predictable "but not too predictable"? I do not know.

"Freedom is relative, but it is entirely freedom, just as a piece of sugar is only a piece, but it is entirely sugar" (qualitative identity but quantitative difference). One might object that this works very well with sugar and with anything else, *except* what we are interested in here, namely the Whole/Nature/God. Being part of the free Whole, which is God, does not imply that we are divine. Why not? Because God (or All or Nature) is the only being whose essence is not to be divided up. In short, when you break sugar into cubes, you still have sugar: the change in quantity has not altered the quality. But when you split up God, you no longer have God, since God's essence is not to be split up: either he is fully himself, or he is not. However, this also leads Spinoza into inextricable contradictions...

You also say: "The usual trap is to imagine determinism as a straight line that crosses the field of possibilities, making everything that is not on that line impossible, whereas determinism is precisely the entire field of possibilities." That is interesting, because Spinoza could say the same thing without concluding, as you do, that this saves "the classical, binary definition of freedom (i.e., 'having a choice')." In fact, all possibilities must be realized, but the order in which they are realized has no reason not to be determined. A potentiality cannot decide to occur on one day rather than another. So there is still no choice.

"Be that as it may, we can see the absurdity of this contemporary desire to define freedom as openness to an infinite number of choices, all of which would be equal, when it is rather a matter of identifying one and only one direction, the right direction": that is very faithful to Spinoza!

I will not go into the political and historical problem, since we would first have to settle the metaphysical question that conditions it.

You might reply: Spinoza is a very special and subtle deterministic thinker, and, all things considered, he agrees with Hegel on many points. Hegel would be a Spinozist without knowing it − or knowing it and admitting it sometimes, not always. And this would be an answer that would suit me.

However, for many reasons, I am neither a Spinozist nor a Hegelian. So far, I have no satisfactory solution to the "problem of determinism and freedom." I lean towards absolute determinism, but only because of the *efficiency* of its results and its *predictive* power. Experimental psychology, for example, can predict "attitudes," states of consciousness. I do not have a strong *argument* to defend it, given that I do not believe, unlike most scientists, either in materialist reductionism or in the principle of causality − so I cannot turn to them to defend absolute determinism, if it is true.

Congratulations again on your excellent work in popularizing this matter.

L. F.

First Response


So, if I understand what you mean:

I spoke very briefly about the criticism of determinism in the strict sense, because this position is untenable, precisely because it calls for the lazy argument, which in itself shatters strict determinism: in fact, as you say, being determined does not imply having no choice. What I am criticizing here is the "naïve" determinism that comes before the lazy argument. Perhaps I should have said, "...such advice *would* be totally unhelpful on their part since, *according to them* (strict determinists), man (supposedly) has no choice, neither to accept nor to refuse something." That would have been clearer. It seems to me that the lazy argument is not a solution for determinism, but precisely an admission of weakness that forces us to imply the decision, and, therefore, to introduce freedom into determinism. This is what I said further on: the fact that my decision is guided by previous external causes does not take away from the fact that I am the one who decides, I am the one who acts, so freedom (however imperfect, relative, etc.) is already there. In fact, we are already in the dialectic: you are suggesting that this freedom is a constraint, a determinism. *Yes*, but the opposite is also true. To say "we are free to be determined" is to say "we are determined to be free." At least, throughout the rest of the presentation, I try to demonstrate this...

"You must not mix the point of view of the Whole with that of the part." I try not to mix them, not to merge them either, but to dialecticize them! The part and the whole... It is like relative and absolute: you have to understand the dialectical nature of the thing. Of course, we must not confuse the parts with the whole. They are very different, while being the same thing – the parts are the parts of the whole, and the whole is itself only by virtue of the parts. It is only in a non-dialectical approach that the whole and the parts are (wrongly) totally distinguishable. In the dialectical approach, contradiction is recognized, and the thing is apprehended by understanding the contradiction working within it... Similarly, the relative is already the absolute "without really being so;" it is the absolute "in itself," which becomes more and more "absolutized" as it tends towards the "absolute" – which, incidentally, will never eliminate the relative, which will forever remain a component, a moment of the absolute. At no point does the relative exist outside its link to the absolute, and vice versa – it is a logical impossibility. You are never in one place and then the other; you switch from one point of view to another... There is not a moment of "filling up" the relative (at 73.2%, for example, or even 100%) when it would cease to be relative and suddenly become absolute. Even the very relative is already absolute, while not being so! In essence, they are one.

This is why it is not so much a question of knowing how to germinate a little freedom in determinism: it is more a matter of grasping how to establish a difference (always relative) between the two. By "absolutizing" the relative, we do not so much obtain a freer freedom as a freedom more in tune with determinism, and ultimately, a more coherent world. For Marx, in a world where men were emancipated and happy, they would not ask themselves whether they were *free to be happy* or *determined to be happy*. It would not matter that much. The question itself is a form of alienation, *stemming from* alienation in the broadest sense, and resolved through social emancipation. Hegel may be less optimistic, but he still sees this inclination towards a balance between freedom and determinism in the rational state. In both cases, it is a contradiction that needs to be resolved. Until then, the contradiction is there: the whole and the parts, the relative and the absolute, etc., *appear* as two different things – and this is real, not an illusion. But, at all times, relative and absolute (or "whole and parts," "freedom and determinism") are in essence one and the same thing.

Consciousness is already freedom *as a principle*. Of course, alienated consciousness (in consciousness or practice, it is the same) is less free, but it is already free – for example, in the dialectic of master and slave, at any moment the slave may prefer to rebel, even if it means dying. This is also a reference to La Boétie: "Resolve to serve no more..." Hegel's point is precisely that there is no need for proof: it is more a matter of defining the concept.

By the way, are determinists asked to prove determinism? Hardly. Even when they do provide "proof," it is according to *their* self-validating definition, which is just as much a postulate as freedom. On the other hand, when confronted with "libertinists," we do not hesitate to call all their arguments postulates! I believe there is a real ideological bias, a scientistic (and rather deterministic) postulate that dominates our times, whereby we ask the latter for proofs that we will always reject before they give it to us, while we consider the postulates of the former as implicit proofs... This is what I call (pejoratively) "wanting to *start from determinism*."

Hegel (curiously enough) calls "chemism" the "truth of mechanism," i.e., the fact that, when the mechanism is brought face to face with itself (one object against another), we move from action to reaction, and find that cause and effect are interchangeable – is it the wind that moves the tree branches, or do the tree branches deflect the wind's course? If you want to keep the word mechanism, why not, but mechanism does not mean determinism any *more* than freedom does... It is always a matter of "point of view."

I do not know much about quantum physics and its challenges, but I am inclined to think that, whatever comes of it, it will not upset Hegel, who, once again, takes a philosophical rather than a scientific approach, so he is mainly interested in language, in the very definitions of the words we use. He approaches the question through the concept, which overrides the scientific approach. But since I know more about philosophy than mathematics or physics, it is perhaps a form of arrogance on my part to deny the latter a metaphysical status...

You write: "Likewise, one could at least assume that we are externally determined to 'internalize determinism'": yes, we certainly are, but here are two things that must be said:

- First, the moment of internalization, by being a moment of appropriation, turns determinism into freedom.

- Second, there is (once again) a dialectic of inside and outside. They too are one in the absolute. The world around us is an extension of ourselves, just as we are an extension of it. So even when the "outside" determines us, it is still we who determine ourselves (which is freedom), *since* the world is also us. We are also the divine that determines. If we are puppets, we are also puppeteers, since the universe is not foreign to us, it is us and we are it – or at least we must strive for that unity. I will return to this point.

What I call open or closed causality is, let us say... Imagine you throw a small cube of wood on the table. This results in a small wooden cube on the table. Now, if you write a number on each side, and throw it again, you will get (additionally) a number from 1 to 6. And only humans write numbers on cubes... We do not choose the result of the dice, but we choose to throw it... It is consciousness that, *through choice* (regardless of whether or not it is "externally caused" beforehand), breaks a linear, mechanistic movement in the strict sense, to move towards an "open" mechanism that opens up a variety of possibilities. In nature, there is no wood. Only trees exist. With consciousness, we now have wood, and thanks to it the dice, the table, the house, the paper, the book, all of these being results of man's freedom – and you may tell me that this is determinism rather than freedom, but I would still say that deep down (in essence) it is the same... I might even add, at the risk of being wrong, that it is a conditioned reflex, due to our times, that makes you spontaneously look for determinism behind every freedom, *rather than the opposite.*

On the question of the fragmentation of God, I think the objection is not valid. God *can* be fragmented, and can even *only* be fragmented – see the whole that exists only through its parts. Once again, we must dialecticize to the end. God is not (at least with Hegel, I am not sure about Spinoza) something other than the world, he is the world. God is fully himself only in the whole, but the whole is nothing other than the parts, properly understood. Once again, there is no abrupt shift between the relative and the absolute. We are *already* the divine, but the divine is weakened and alienated by its contradictions – both theoretical and practical – yet to be resolved. If "Deus sive Natura," then we may not be God (the whole), but we are entirely *made of* the divine – as in the example of sugar. Or to put it another way: if God's *essence* is not to be fragmented, his *existence* is to be fragmented.

It seems to me that all possibilities are determined, but that *the* possibility chosen by a consciousness is an act of freedom – that is what I meant. And what is more, this choice will immediately turn into determinism for future choices to be made! So determinism and freedom are constantly turning into each other... I think Sartre would say something close to this, namely that freedom consists in having a total choice but in a totally predetermined situation – The same happens with Marx when he affirms that men make history but in circumstances made by history. What is superior about Hegel compared to Sartre, in my opinion, is that Hegel shows that you are not determined (*and only determined*) on Monday, then free (*and only free*) on Tuesday: you are free and determined at every moment, all the time. Freedom and determinism are a contradiction (to be grasped as such), not metaphysical options among which we should spot the true one.

"That is very faithful to Spinoza!" Indeed, I am less familiar with Spinoza, but perhaps 80% of Hegel is already in Spinoza, just as 80% of Spinoza is probably already in his predecessors – so goes history... Hegel knows very well what he owes to Spinoza, but he enriches it, especially with the "passage from substance to subject," from determinism to freedom. My main interest in Hegel is that he corrects Spinoza (when necessary), whereas the reverse is obviously not possible. But that is laziness on my part, a faulty shortcut, because Spinoza, of course, deserves to be studied for himself...

I will conclude. In my opinion, as far as I understand it (but I do not claim to have the ultimate truth, nor even a true understanding of Hegel), freedom and determinism are a problem only for non-dialectical thinking, and dialectics solves the problem entirely *in theory*, i.e., you can spend a lifetime exploring the question, but the main solution is this: freedom and determinism are one and the same thing, whose contradictory relationship with itself must be understood. Hegel wrote, when faced with the "problem of mind and body interaction" (in Descartes): "The question was asked in such a way that it became impossible to solve it." By this, he meant that, from the moment we consider body and mind (or freedom and determinism, subject and object, relative and absolute, etc.) as two different things, they will forever pose a problem because only the dialectical approach (properly understood) allows us not to move forward, but to elucidate the question once and for all. I know it seems crazy to think that Hegel would have solved the problem two centuries ago and that today's philosophers and scientists would ignore it for some reason... But let me tell you something: I watched a recent video by "Monsieur Phi" on the question of freedom and determinism. He does not mention Hegel or dialectics even once – unless I was sneezing when he did! He refers to numerous recent studies by "specialists," almost turning the subject into a political-democratic question ("According to you, are you free in such a situation? Vote to see who wins"!), and he mentions "compatibilist" theories that argue that freedom and determinism could be "mixed"... But that is just like Descartes, who looked for the link between body and mind in the "pineal gland" – which is part of the body, and therefore resolves nothing. The only serious way of approaching this question is as follows: body and mind are one and the same thing, *whose contradiction must be considered.* Matter is incarnated spirit, and spirit is spiritualized matter. We go around and around in circles trying to "decide" in favor of one or the other – the chicken and the egg... The same applies to the question of freedom and determinism. The starting point is the dialectical unity of the two, and this is what I try to explain in all my videos, which have just one goal, whatever the subject is: to help people move from understanding to reason, from binary and formal thinking to dialectical thinking. Either I am crazy and have not understood a thing (which is not impossible), or it is just staggering to see how many "philosophers" continue to pose a dialectical question in a binary way, relying on a thousand works by other people who do the same. I have nothing against "Monsieur Phi," who is a very nice person by the way, but to miss the essential point in a 53-minute video, and then have the nerve to call it "Philosophers do not understand anything about freedom," it is a bit strong.

I can see from the comments under my videos that some people find it difficult to understand. I have not yet succeeded in getting across this one and only message: to explain in a simple way what dialectics is... but one day I will!

Thank you for this discussion,

L. M.

Second message

Thank you for your answer, which is so exhaustive. I continue the discussion as it interests me for my own journey. You often come very close to refuting me, which helps me move forward.

I am not sure I understand your response to the lazy argument. "It seems to me that the lazy argument is not a solution for determinism": in fact, it is precisely conceived as an objection to determinism, to which some determinists have tried to respond.

Without the need for dialectics, Spinoza would translate "we are determined to be free" as "we are determined to strive to determine ourselves." For example, man is "constrained" by his nature to strive for a vaccine. Here, Spinoza sounds anachronistically like Hegel. But there is a big difference: Spinoza will always say "strive" only, and never "man can entirely determine himself," because only the Whole is capable of that. Which logically leads to the next point.

I think I am roughly familiar with the dialectic of whole and part – if it agrees with that of the infinite and the finite. But I would like to point out two things:

a) I recognize that, logically, the Whole and the part are both the same thing and absolutely different – like pure Being and nothingness. But let us return to our most everyday human experience. It is all very well to show logically that, from a certain point of view, the whole and the part are one and the same, but does that mean that everything we say about the whole can be said about the part? Since "the world is both totally determined and totally free" (I agree with this proposition), can I also say that "the individual is both totally determined and totally free"? That would run counter to our everyday human experience: I feel limited on all sides; the freedom of a simple bacterium can negate my own... If I had the same freedom as the infinity of reality, this bacterium could not negate my freedom.

I now see what the answer to this might be: as an individual-part, being involved in the freedom of the Whole does imply that I have the determining power of the universe, but the power of the Whole is itself limited, because the Whole has to become part, which is why my power or freedom is limited.

However, it does seem to me, for example, that my individual freedom is inferior to the freedom of the solar system – for instance, I die if I go into the cosmic void. How can we explain this? How can we explain that one part of the universe (me) does not *also* have the freedom of another part (the solar system), even though both the solar system and I are also parts of the Whole, and *we are both the Whole as parts*?

b) Now, here is a rather important remark about dialectics in general. I am going to venture not just to criticize Hegel, but to propose something more, positively. I am completely convinced when Hegel demonstrates that categories give birth to their own contradiction – the infinite is and is not the finite, etc. However, once this demonstration has been made, it seems to me that coming out of it smiling, proud of an "accepted contradiction," is quite astonishing. At the end of dialectical reasoning (e.g., the Whole and the Part), it is no longer clear whether it is even possible to continue talking. Why do I say "part" when the part is the whole? Should I say "partwhole"? No, because it is also true that the part is not the whole. So I will say "partwholebutnotwhole." In short, I am either crazy or silent – I am thinking of Aristotle concerning this way of criticizing the violation of the principle of non-contradiction. Nothing to get excited about! It is better to return to the principle of non-contradiction, but not because it is true! – as Aristotle wrongly thought. Truth is indeed contradictory and Hegel is right. However, we must return to the principle of non-contradiction and thus live in *falsehood*, so that we keep living – and not even "live in falsehood," since that would again initiate a dialectic of true and false, but rather live by somehow forgetting this dialectic.

In summary, it seems to me that, in many respects, Hegel has *rigorously* destroyed philosophy. Dialectics is a rigorous demonstration of the failure of thought. It is the realization that thought, by digging into itself, and the world itself too, since thought and the world are linked, have no meaning, are unthinkable and unnameable, and even these words must be avoided (for being comes from nothingness, etc.), we should just be silent. Hegel has demonstrated the absurdity of the world.

More debatable now, from a naturalistic perspective: our categories logically give birth to their own contradiction, because they were never meant to be investigated as rigorously as Hegel's genius did. Hegel finds the illogical by exploring logic, for it is illogical for a living being to want to explore logic – because this probably leads to silence or madness, not action. Hegel discovers that our categories transgress the principle of non-contradiction, because they were not made to be coherent, but simply to give us the *impression* of logic.

As you can see, I am not criticizing dialectics, but rather what Hegel does with dialectics. It seems to me that Hegelian truth leads to what Hegel hates so much, namely the unspeakable.

I completely agree with you about the postulates of determinists *and* libertinists: irrationality versus irrationality. Then comes Hegel, whose merit is to rigorously exacerbate irrationality.

And to answer the question as to why we are most attracted today to the irrationality of determinism: there is the influence of a scientistic ideology indeed, but also the fact that determinism makes it possible to *predict* phenomena. It seems to me that this predictive power should not be overlooked. That does not make determinism true! But can we say that an idea is "knowledge" when it does not allow us to predict? We have little interest in a knowledge of freedom, because knowledge without its predictive power may not be knowledge at all. Hegel could, if necessary, identify tendencies (historical trends, in particular, although I do not really believe in them, but that is another matter), but the fact remains that humanity, at any time, can take the "wrong" path, so no predictions are possible.

I follow you on chemism – or rather you taught me something about Hegel.

Then you write: "First, the moment of internalization, by being a moment of appropriation, turns determinism into freedom." Then consciousness can realize that its very act of appropriation was externally determined (a return to determinism) – for example, consciousness conceiving the possibility of being in a Putnam-like vat. But then consciousness can *appropriate* this new determinism, and thereby "return" to freedom! Then consciousness may think that this appropriation of this new determinism is itself determined from the outside by a second machine... And so on. We fall into what seems to me to be the *sterility* inherent in dialectics. That is why it is quite simple to conclude that living in a computer simulation or not *makes no difference.* And you do the same when you say later on in the (good) example of the dice: whether we place ourselves at the level of determinism or freedom, it really makes no difference. *Hegelianism is the demonstration of this fundamental undecidability.* It is very impressive. But there is nothing to be thrilled about!

About the end of your answer, I would say again that Hegel's argument is very good (that is why I am more of a Hegelian than a Spinozist, I also think Hegel "corrected" Spinozism, as you said), but then I would come back to the question of what to do with the Hegelian demonstration once we have subscribed to it.

Regarding the "Monsieur Phi" video, I totally agree that Hegel has been ignored, and thinkers act as if he were out of date. The "experimental philosophy" you describe does not deserve the name philosophy, in my opinion. And many English-speaking philosophers disregard the history of philosophy and believe that philosophical problems will be solved scientifically... without realizing that the scientific approach is itself a philosophy – often a naive one. So you are much closer to the truth (if it makes sense to say that) than many contemporary thinkers and philosophers. "Monsieur Phi" ignores or underestimates Hegel because his main inspirations do the same – analytic philosophy and formal logic.

I also thank you for this discussion, through which I discover or refine ideas. If the same happens to you, do not hesitate to contact me again.


L. F.

Second Response

Yes, my mistake, I misunderstood the meaning of the lazy argument.

You write: "I recognize that, logically, the Whole and the part are both the same thing and absolutely different." However, to be precise, I think it would be more accurate to say that the Whole and the part are both the same thing and *relatively* different. It is only "absolutely" (in the absolute) that they are not different.

You criticize the statement that "the individual is both totally determined and totally free," but I think we can support it. He is totally determined and totally free "in the absolute of his relativity," "in the absolute of his part," if that sentence can make sense. In the general principle of his life, he is both totally determined and totally free. But, *from a certain point of view*, he is freer at one place than another, more determined at one moment than another, or regarding that attribute or another...

We could perhaps try to explore the question of freedom through one aspect of the problem: responsibility. To take your example of the bacterium that determines you (that makes you sick), you are at the same time totally free to fight against the disease by treating yourself, or to carry out scientific research to make progress in medicine, or to wait for it to pass, or to let yourself die, etc. You are totally free in your *reaction*. Besides, even the bacteria *come from you*, or at least the illness caused by the bacteria, comes from you. It is *your body* that is sick, not the bacteria. Your suffering is *your* suffering before it is your suffering *caused* by this or that. Your life (your own body) is the primary cause of your suffering. Hegel says: "To be able to drink, one must be *capable of thirst*" – or again: "To die is the *privilege* of the living." This, by the way, is what makes people responsible for their actions. Otherwise, it is too easy to always blame the outside world for what we do not like, as you do when you consider bacteria as an external constraint. To take another example, we can complain about not finding a job by saying that "society is bad," when it is perhaps also the lack of skill and effort on the part of the person concerned that is to blame. Besides, society is what we make of it. I know it sounds far-fetched when Hegel asserts, for example, that "when the individual dies, he dies of himself," but this is the general (and necessary) concept, which is only refined and relativized in a later stage. First of all, in absolute terms, the individual is totally free and responsible; Then, in a second stage, this responsibility is divided and relativized when confronted with another individual – or another circumstance. But even if someone kills me, I am free, not in the sense that I would have chosen to die (freedom is not omnipotence, just as absolute knowledge is not omniscience), but in the sense that they could have killed me because I was a man (whose flesh is easily cut by the blade of a knife), in a world that I *know* is violent. And what did I do to avoid being killed? Nothing. I did not take a self-defense course, I did not hire a bodyguard, I did not commit suicide or lock myself away to make sure I would not be killed, etc. I am not just me, I am me in the world, a world full of killers and bacteria. So, if I am ill, I am not determined by something external (outside the world), but by this me-in-the-world, whose responsibility it is to understand risks and to act in advance of the catastrophe to prevent it. And if a disease or an assassin kills me, it is not *unfair*. It is a *pity*. If society then has its legitimate reasons to imprison the killer, etc., it does not take away from the fact that I was free from the beginning to the end of my life. Perhaps humanity will one day invent the means for the individual to be immortal, but, precisely: our freedom lies in finding that technology and that medicine, if we want it, and if we do not find it, or not yet, it is not the world's fault but our own. It all sounds cruel and harsh, but it allows everyone to be held accountable – including the killer, who, otherwise, could *also* say: "Don't condemn me, *I was not free*, it was temporary insanity..." In short, it is a very unhealthy reflection (which we all have, it is the trap Hegel calls the "beautiful soul") to see evil as "determining us" and good as "our free action," which comes down to saying: "The problem is other people, *I* am a good person!" This is why we need to be wary of our "human experience," our feelings. Because we have the feeling (or point of view) that corresponds to our interest, both on the question of freedom and on the others. Understanding the concept of freedom allows us to see things clearly, and stop using the issue as an opportunity for all our hypocrisies.

That said (and to return from responsibility to freedom itself), before being a moral issue, it is a technical question of defining the concept. Grasping the concept of freedom, in all its facets, is complex. Freedom is not simply a concept, but a concept that contains many others, all of which interact with and transform one another... You have to patiently "reconstruct" the concept of freedom in your head, and not ask for a ready-made solution in one sentence – such as: "Are we free? Yes or no, tick the corresponding box"... Don't forget that Hegel said that a result is always the synthesis that gathers and brings together *all the pathways* that lead to the result... If you are a bit lost (and so am I), it is because freedom is often confused with one of its "moments," one of its facets.

You say: "I now see what the answer to this might be: as an individual-part, being involved in the freedom of the Whole implies that I have the determining power of the universe, but the power of the Whole is itself limited because the Whole has to become a part, which is why my power or freedom is limited." That is exactly it. You have a perfect and complete power, but only *of what you are* – with your qualities and flaws. And when you fall ill, you are no longer the healthy you of yesterday. You are already, *immediately*, this new sick you, with his perfect freedom to react to this new situation that is you.

You also say: "However, it seems to me, for example, that my individual freedom is inferior to the freedom of the solar system – for instance, because of the experience of death if I go into the cosmic void. How can we explain this? How can we explain that one part of the universe (me) does not also have the freedom of another part (the solar system), even though both the solar system and I are parts of the Whole, and we are both the Whole as parts?" Here, two things:

- First of all, you yourself answered this question in the previous sentence ("Now I see..."): the parts are all parts with the same "ontological status" as parts, but there are parts that are "bigger" than others, parts stronger than others and, in this respect, parts that are "freer" than others. But each of these parts is completely free by itself. A tiny "part" may have less freedom, but it is entirely free to use its faculties, no matter how small they may be. You and I do not have the same qualities and flaws, but each of us is free to do *what we want and can* with our *own* lives. It is the *principle*, the *concept* of freedom, which is infinite. In practice, freedom is "relativized" by no longer being just freedom (in general), but your freedom or my freedom. But here again, we must not forget the dialectics of the relative and the absolute: the relative is a part of the absolute, so it is entirely *some* absolute. If I may put it this way, I would say that freedom as a quality is always infinite, but freedom also always has *a quantity that is finite*. I do not know if that is a correct way to say it

- Second, it seems to me that you are infinitely freer than the Sun, even through the experience of death – "to die is the *privilege* of the living." The Sun will never die, because it will never have *lived*. It will have *been*, it will have *burned*, then it will have *disappeared*. All in an empty space. You will have *lived, existed, smelled, tasted, touched, spoken, listened, loved, suffered, hoped,* and *meditated* on your existence in a living, infinitely complex world... You will have *enjoyed the Sun*, which does not even enjoy itself... Finally, you will have experienced death – well, not that actually, because, as Epicurus says, when we are dead, we no longer experience anything.

This despair you mention, which leads to silence or madness, is not the result of dialectics but, on the contrary, the result of non-dialectics – binary understanding. Heraclitus (as I understand it) was tormented by the fact that theses turned into antitheses, because he was looking for synthesis, he was looking for *the whole* without reaching it. Pyrrho, on the other hand, chose to make this failure a positive outcome: he decided that nothing had to be chosen, since "everything was valid." It was because dialectics was confusing, in its infancy, that we could not make it to the end. It was Hegel who, much later, succeeded in making the dialectics clear – so to speak! And dialectics provides a clear answer, not an undecidable vagueness that drives people mad or hopeless.

There is the thesis. Which leads to the antithesis. Finally, and most difficult to grasp, the synthesis. What is the synthesis? It is this act of "overcome conservation", that clarifies the well-understood relationship between thesis and antithesis – their well-understood relationship of unity and difference, of difference in unity and unity in difference. To go back again to the example of the whole and the parts: there is the part, considered (incorrectly) abstractly – "the kingdom within a kingdom." There is the whole, considered (incorrectly) abstractly – the whole as an "empty shell," as a self-sufficient thing not composed of other things. Then there is the synthesis, namely: we understand that every part is necessarily part of a whole (so it is not by itself, it is by something else, by its opposite) and that the whole is nothing other than its parts taken together – the whole too is what it is only thanks to its opposite, the parts. So, each being only through the other, each being defined by the other, it can be said to be one and the same thing, or rather one and the same *contradiction*. But they are one thing in essence and two things in existence. The truth of synthesis is that there are three things: the parts, the whole, and the whole-parts. Synthesis is an overcoming, but also a *preservation* that does not kill thesis and antithesis. It acknowledges the contradiction, not in a "smiling and proud" way, but rather in a permanent effort – intellectual effort for theory, and social effort for practice, in particular.

What you may be missing to fully understand is the notion of *historicity* – or processuality. Hegel does not destroy philosophy; on the contrary, he accomplishes it. Or at least tries to. You cannot blame dialectics (or Hegel) for killing thought, because it is actually what makes thought possible, through the solution of contradiction. The criticism leveled at dialectics or Hegel (by Kierkegaard, for example, but also by many others) is not that it creates confusion (that is Heraclitus) or undecidability (that is Pyrrho). The criticism leveled at dialectics or Hegel is that, by acknowledging the contradiction, dialectics postpones until tomorrow the solution to the contradiction. Marx, for example, is criticized for the fact that his dialectical theory is proven by the advent of the classless society... *which we are still waiting for*! Likewise, in Hegel, the completion of philosophy (and I mean completion, not destruction) is always for tomorrow, we do not see the end of this process since we are still in contradiction. Dialectical philosophy is the only coherent philosophy, because it can prove everyone right: far from destroying other philosophies or despising them, *it welcomes them* all into the final system, each in its rightful place. But this system is only fully coherent at the very end. Until then, there is still contradiction, and what does contradiction do? It whispers in our ears: "It is so hard to keep this contradiction at arm's length! Aren't you tired? Would not it be easier to choose sides? Look at this thesis! Isn't it attractive? Or how about this antithesis? Isn't it convincing? I do not care which one you choose, but *you have to choose, so that you live and rely on something solid.*" Solid, yes, but *abstract*, i.e. *false*, or at least partially true... The only problem with dialectics is that it offers truth and emancipation *for tomorrow* – as a task to be accomplished, not as a cake to be enjoyed. Until then, as the days or centuries go by, we move forward or backward, towards a more softened contradiction (progress of history) or an exacerbated one (period of decline)... But if we "firmly hold" the contradiction (an expression Hegel likes to use), we have the promise of truth in the making, and we can see it looming on the horizon although we cannot touch it. What creates despair or madness, on the contrary, is not to consider synthesis, but to go from thesis to antithesis *ad infinitum*, without end, since both are true at the same time. This is not dialectics, but the absence (or refusal) of dialectics.

In the perfect world at the end of history, the whole and the part are *really* one, because they harmonize perfectly – society and individuals no longer tear each other apart, but merge into a harmonious whole. But today, for now, the whole and parts are one in essence, but *two in existence*: a contradiction we experience as *pain*. Historicity, the dynamic of time, the becoming of contradiction, is fundamental to understanding what we are talking about: the world is never totally coherent or totally incoherent – it is caught between these two extremes. It becomes, it constantly changes, towards higher or lower degrees of coherence. Parts tear each other apart (in war, for example), or on the contrary, they *make* the whole, bring it to life – through knowledge, love, harmony...

So there are the parts (abstraction), the whole (also abstraction), and the parts and the whole *as they seek to achieve their unity through time* (concrete synthesis). We need to master these different stages, which are the absolute opposite of a shapeless mess where everything is mixed together...

Dialectics is the opposite of "the rigorous demonstration of the failure of thought." It is the rigorous demonstration of the triumph of thought, *provided we understand what exactly thought is*. Hegel does not demonstrate the absurdity of the world. In my opinion, he is the most successful at making sense of it.

You write: "We have little interest in a knowledge of freedom, because knowledge without its predictive power may not be knowledge at all." Precisely, freedom is closely linked to knowledge, which has indeed a predictive power. The predictive power of knowledge *allows* freedom. Being able to forecast the weather gives me the freedom to plan my weekend based on the weather.

That being said, predicting history is another matter... We may doubt our ability to predict history, but it is also the most important thing we need to know, because history in the broadest sense is what conditions everything else in our lives. Human emancipation will not be made possible by weather forecasts... Even the vaguest knowledge of history, even haphazard forecasts, are precious and indispensable. Once again, in my opinion, dialectic is fertility itself. On the contrary, it is binary thinking that goes around and around in undecidability. Only dialectics *and history* can save us from despair and sterility.

As to what to do with dialectics once you have embraced it: use it! Put it into theory and practice. Think with it, through it, follow the train of contradiction (which allows us to envisage its solution), then act according to the results obtained.


L. M.

Third message

You were right to want to keep these messages public on your channel because, against all odds, we have a reader. It gets a bit complicated if I try to reply to A. at the same time, so for now I will just say telegraphically:

- Yes, I sometimes have Wittgenstein in mind, on his use of meaning, his idea of the "hardness of the soft," which I link to Popper and his "building erected on piles," to say that scientific "progress" is necessarily built partly with falsehood (or rather with the unthought) that must be considered *as if* it were solid.

- So far, I think we have managed to avoid the dialogue of the deaf. Even if at the end of this exchange we were to stand firm on our positions, they would each have been strengthened by having passed the test of objections. This is only possible, of course, if the objections have been rationally formulated, and that seems to me to be the case at the moment.

- "You say that it would be better to abandon dialectics (the speculative, reason) and part with the principle of non-contradiction, or even stop thinking... I do not see how one could defend this..." Strictly speaking, in fact, it is impossible to "defend" the cessation of thought, since such a defense would presuppose thought. What does seem possible, however, is to attempt to defend the opposite, and to realize that the most rational thought (Hegel's) somehow leads to the sterility of thought. And it would be thought itself that would lead to this conclusion. But I will try to be clearer in what follows. It is not the result of years of reflection. It is just an attempt to read into Hegel some intuitions I have had for a long time, and which do not come exclusively from any one author.

I am replying to L. M.'s message now. You know Hegel very well, better than I, and above all you have a rather extraordinary gift for explaining him in layman's terms, offering examples that would take me much longer to find.

I will start by answering the remark about the Sun, although at some point it might make us go slightly off-topic. I feel quite comfortable admitting that I have a kind of spiritual superiority over the Sun. Here, I am thinking of Kant and his idea of the sublime, whose inspiration is probably Pascal's thinking reed. However, you seem to have decided to insist on the "thinking" side of man, when we should just as much insist on the fact that he is just a reed, he can be crushed at any time – in short, the idea of human finitude. From this point of view, the Sun seems more powerful than me. To say purely and simply that I would be "infinitely freer than the Sun" seems to me a strange kind of freedom, when, however, I am being compared to something that certainly does not think, does not exist, and is not aware of itself – although, to be more precise, it seems to me that the Sun is *less* aware of itself, and that there are different degrees of awareness, because when we see that the elephant recognizes itself in a mirror, that the gorilla Koko used language (signs and not just signals like bees), we end up assuming that there is a *continuum* from consciousness to the absence of consciousness. Anyway, getting back to my sentence: my "infinite freedom" seems very strange to me when it comes to comparing myself to a star, i.e., something that remains in existence for billions of years, can sustain the life of an entire planet, contains an energy unimaginably greater than my own, and that, following its potential implosion into a supernova, can become a black hole that perhaps leads to other dimensions of the universe.

This idea of finitude (the "reed" side of man) is partly found in Hegel, as you remind us: the hour of our birth is the hour of our death. However, it also seems to me that the Sun is a little *less* finite than I am – for the reasons mentioned above, let us say its raw power and not its degree of self-awareness. It would be important to prove that things are *more or less finite*. But this seemed difficult to prove following Hegel, so I asked: how can I understand that the Sun is a greater part of the Whole than I am, whereas the Sun and I are *both the Whole* insofar as the Whole must express itself through parts? (If you answer that the Sun is a greater part of the Whole than I am, because he is the Whole insofar as the Whole must express itself through parts that are greater than I am, then this would just be a tautology, a sleeping virtue of opium to explain that it makes you sleep).

In your attempt to answer this question, you recognized the necessity of saying: "parts are all parts with the same "ontological status" as parts, but there are parts that are "bigger" than others, parts that are stronger than others and, in this respect, parts that are "freer" than others." But then you do not set out the Hegelian argument that would prove this. Hegel probably answers this when he deals with quantity in the *Science of Logic* (since what is at issue is the finitude of quantity, according to you), but I have not sufficiently explored this section yet. If you ever do a presentation on quantity in *Logic*, I would love to hear it.

You have also tried to answer this problem by arguing that "the Whole and the Part are both the same thing and *relatively* different." However, first of all, I find it hard to understand how two things could be relatively different without also being *relatively* the same; secondly, on the topic of pure Being and nothingness, Hegel does write that they are "absolutely different," but perhaps this is specific to this section. I have just read an article by a certain Franz Grégoire, who lists different meanings of contradiction or "supersession" in Hegel's Logic, depending on the passage from the Logic that we consider[45].

You write: "The individual is totally determined and totally free 'in the absolute of his relativity', 'in the absolute of his part', if that phrase can make sense." This sentence probably does not "make sense" and that is probably because it is absolutely true.

I am with you on the subject of responsibility and bacteria, although what would interest me, even more, is to know the extent to which the bacteria is *not* me, as well as a way of determining that degree of difference. Otherwise, we fall into confusion: since the killer cannot kill me without me, since he and I are dialectically linked, since my interior is violated only as it necessarily relates to the exterior, since I am, so to speak, "in" the killer so that he can kill me, then, when he kills me, he makes me live, because I live in the killer who kills me! Could this be some kind of suicide? And, since the killer is killing a person in whom, to kill it, he must logically be in, is he killing himself as well? Is this a double suicide? Yet, at the end of the day, we will see a living person and a dead person. Besides, you can see how the study of any particular example (murder, bacteria...) becomes complex through dialectics. But how can we *act* when faced with such complexities? Nothing could be more obscure in my eyes than your suggestion to "use" dialectics, "to act according to the result obtained." By the way, a sign of the difficulty of acting with Hegel, or rather a sign of what I called this undecidability: don't we find it in the fact that, two hundred years after Hegel, there are as many right-wing Hegelians as

---

[45] Grégoire Franz, "Hegel et l'universelle contradiction", *Revue philosophique de Louvain*, vol. 44, 1946, p. 36-73.

left-wing Hegelians as there are centrist Hegelians, even though there are still some attentive readers of Hegel among them?

You yourself say: "It was Hegel who, much later, succeeded in making the dialectics in a clear way – so to speak! And dialectics provides a clear answer (...)". But if it is so difficult to understand, perhaps it is because it is really not clear. Or rather, dialectics is difficult to *express*, because you seem to have understood certain Hegelian dialectics very well, and I think I have understood some of them, but we cannot really express them clearly, and I am not sure this is due to the weakness of our intellects.

This brings me to the most important point. You underline the fact that Hegel did not simply show the internal contradiction of all things (and thus the madness proper to reason and the absurdity proper to the world, so to speak), for this contradiction is both the act of overcoming and preserving (the famous "Aufhebung"), it is not a destructive force but a constructive, driving one. It is to this point that I must respond.

I will take an example from the beginning of the *Logic*: the "overcoming" of being-in-itself and being-for-others in the contradictory concept of "limit." Hegel has shown that every "something" has both a necessary link to others (its being-for-others) and a kind of core impervious to others – the being-in-itself, which makes the something and its other not one and the same thing. Then he points out that there is a concept that embraces both these properties, the concept of limit: indeed, the limit delimits what is within it (a being-in-itself), but it also points towards what goes beyond the limit (being-for-others); the limit is this boundary, this in-between. But is it because we have at hand a word ("limit"), or rather an oft-used concept, that we have *overcome* being-for-others and being-in-itself, and not simply *juxtaposed* these two terms into a single one, which thus *conceals* the painfulness of the contradiction? The limit means nothing else than the fact of being both in oneself and for others, so we have not made any progress at all, since we already knew that every thing has these two properties.

I have the impression that Hegel says: "You see, we find this good old concept of 'limit,' very frequently used, so it is not frightening, the contradiction was not just a destructive formal contradiction! We are not dealing with a contradiction that is driving us mad, and the proof is that we use this concept of limit very peacefully on an almost daily basis. It has a purpose, it is used in the construction of buildings, maps, and so on. So we have made progress in our analysis, we have overcome the contradiction." But then Hegel would be forgetting something very simple: when we talk about daily limits, when we use them to construct buildings, or even mathematics, we are always *forgetting* the fact that it is a contradictory concept. What enables us to live and think daily, specifically, is not the contradictory truth of the concept, but the forgetting of the contradictory truth of the concept. It seems to me that anyone who would always maintain in his speech that being-in-itself presupposes being-for-others, and vice versa, would no longer be able to speak. Humans have created the concept of limit to continue speaking, to forget what the concept of limit *conceals*, namely the contradiction that would make speech impossible.

You write: "This despair you mention, which leads to silence or madness, is not the result of dialectics but, on the contrary, the result of non-dialectics – of binary under-standing." However, I assure you once again that this is dialectics. The point is this: when you start to become aware of the contradictory aspect of understanding, you take your first step into *dialectics*, and you take your first step *out of understanding*. Understanding is not contradiction, understanding is the belief that there is no real contradiction – Kant is the thinker of understanding who *comfortably* takes a walk every morning and believes in the rational basis of morality. To live according to the understanding is to live without realizing the contradiction at work within it – since Kant claims to *resolve* the antinomies of reason. The contradiction of understanding that leads to madness or silence is the *truth* of understanding, namely dialectics. In other words, when Hegel describes the products of understanding as contradictory, he is already doing so *from the vantage point of dialectics*.

However, as I said before, I completely agree that the thought of understanding is false. It is false, but it does not lead to silence or madness; on the contrary, it enables us to live, because life very much needs false judgments to sustain itself (I am thinking of Nietzsche here), life needs simplifications, rigid categories as well as fictions and lies – here I am thinking of Freud, or plays such as Ibsen's *The Wild Duck*.

Your comment on historicity is interesting, but I am not sure I understand why it is necessary to talk about it to solve the problem we face. Above all, I would have to understand *why* historicity exists (and probably it should not be shown dialectically, otherwise we would fall into circular reasoning: dialectics is a true overcoming by virtue of historicity, historicity is true by virtue of dialectics... which is understood by historicity), why "the whole and the parts are one in *essence*, but two in *existence*," and why they should tend to unite, one day, in existence. Lots of grey areas for me. But I know you do not have the time to say it all, so you probably allow yourself a few leaps in your presentation.

I said: "We have little interest in a knowledge of freedom, because knowledge without its predictive power may not be knowledge at all." You replied: "Precisely, freedom is closely linked to knowledge, which has indeed a predictive power. The predictive power of knowledge enables freedom. Being able to forecast the weather gives me the freedom to plan my weekend based on the weather." I also observe this connection, but without seeing it as a fusion: knowledge helps us to exercise what we call freedom, but this does not yet show that there is a "knowledge of freedom." That is what I wanted to talk about. In your example, it seems to me that knowledge deals with meteorological determinism, but the fact remains that there is no knowledge of my freedom to organize my weekend. At least, I was asking about the feasibility of such knowledge.

Kind regards,


L. F.

Third Response

If the question is "Why is the Sun bigger than me *in size* when we are both the whole?," the answer could be this: identity (of the Whole) needs to negate itself into difference (of the parts), to then find true identity, which is *identity through difference* (the Whole through the parts). The same occurs when logic alienates itself in nature, to recover as spirit. By doing so, identity alienates itself into difference: some parts must be larger, others smaller, and some solid, others gaseous, some mineral, others vegetable or animal, etc., otherwise nothing could exist. A universe composed entirely of organic matter could not sustain itself, could not move, could not live. A universe composed entirely of gas or stone would not be *perceived*, and therefore, *would not exist*. At most, it would just *be*. But I think the central point is really this: the Sun is greater than you *as* a part (regarding quantity) but equal to you *as* the Whole (regarding quality: you are both *from* the whole). That is why it is important to maintain the difference (part ≠ whole) and, at the same time, to maintain-overcome it in identity – the "Whole = part," the "true Whole" synthesis of the Whole and parts.

I will attempt an illustration by taking a somewhat "psychologizing" route. I think the Sun is bigger, but not freer. The Sun, insofar as it is not conscious (or only a little), is only great in terms of quantity – size, longevity... In terms of quality, there is an immense difference between a conscious being and a non-conscious being – or one so little conscious. I believe, like Hegel, that consciousness is the foundation of freedom, even if the Sun does indeed have many other qualities that make it "superior" to us. We are freer than the Sun, and I would even say freer than the elephant. But, and this is important, it does not imply a difference in *dignity*. The degree of consciousness is the degree of freedom – or at least it is deeply linked to it. But as I understand it, what we call *dignity* is that side of ourselves (or of things in general) in which we are all equal (the point of view of the Whole, so to speak), but *on the other hand* we are different in a thousand ways (in our "part" aspect), ways that we should be able to recognize, *without this affecting our dignity*. I have already had talks with people who got angry with me precisely because I refused to grant (or rather to recognize) the fern the same consciousness as the man – for them, it was contempt, a kind of racism. Whereas it seems obvious to me that man has more consciousness and is therefore freer – this criterion of consciousness is from Hegel, I am aware of being totally influenced by him, perhaps too much so, but I believe this criterion to be true. This takes nothing away from the "dignity" of the fern, because all things in the world have the same essence – the Whole, Deus sive natura. That is why I wish no harm to animals or plants, but *without forgetting that there is a hierarchy*: in a building in flames, I would save the baby before the ficus. And I think everyone would do the same. I think there is a psychological and moral aspect to the issue here (which makes it confusing): people want to be nice, so they will defend plants, animals (and why not rocks?), making them uncriticizable, precisely because they're *mixing the whole with the part*. They do not understand that the same thing can have an equal aspect (dignity) and an unequal aspect – other aspects like size, strength, consciousness, and freedom. And yet it is clear: among human beings, some are stronger than others, for example, but this is not a *reason* for the stronger ones to enslave the others. This is how we can link an acceptance of reality (we are different as parts) with the need for harmony – we are all identical in that we are *also* the Whole. Note the word "also": we are *both* the Whole identical to itself and the parts different from each other. The result is not a jumble, but a contradiction of the world that tends towards more harmony or more disharmony – more solution or more contradiction. In a rather harmonious society, the contradiction between the whole and the parts diminishes, until it tends towards disappearance, because the parts work together to form the harmonious Whole. In a society torn apart by conflict, on the other hand, the parts harm each other, while the Whole is no more than a concept (or essence) left in the background, whose absence, omission, or non-fulfillment are deplored by priests or philosophers... And in that, the unrealized Whole remains a goal for the parts to achieve.

So we are unequal in talent, equal in dignity – the parts and the whole. We will never be *just identical* or *just different*. We will always be a connection between the two that can be, depending on the moment, more harmonious (example: peace) or more chaotic (example: war). The problem is that when we say this, we are scorned by left-wingers (who, because of their lack of dialectic, *choose to declare that we are all the same, denying differences*), *and* by right-wingers who, because of the same lack of dialectic, think that *because we are different, this must inevitably lead to relations of power, violence, and domination* – they're forgetting identity.

To risk another example: a rotten apple and a good apple must be ranked in order of importance (every human prefers to eat the good apple), but in the eyes of the Whole, it is still cosmic matter, and this rottenness will satisfy the soil, the worms... For every thing, there is the point of view of identity (the Whole) and the point of view of difference (parts). Here we are comparing a human being with the Sun.

But by what criterion? From what point of view? In terms of longevity, size, and warmth, the Sun is the winner. In terms of consciousness and freedom, humans win. And in terms of "dignity," it is equality. Because it is the Sun that allows you to live, but it is you who contemplates it. It is the Sun that enables life, but it is life that enables the Sun to *make itself useful* to life... Power *needs* a being on which to exert itself. Similarly, the notion of "better than" loses all meaning in the absolute (which appeals to the "humanist," anti-hierarchical left), but has an irreducible importance in the parts – which appeals to the realpolitik right, which rejects the "utopia" of universalism. You always have to think about all points of view together, without choosing anyone – that is what I call "accepting contradiction."

As for the Hegelian argument that would prove the necessity of the existence of parts greater than others, I may have expressed myself poorly in the previous message, but I think I have just answered the question: Parts are all parts, but they are different. Trees are all trees, but there are oaks, willows, etc., just as things are all things, but there are willows, planets, insurance companies, nets... Generally speaking, parts are all parts, but *only* regarding what I (clumsily) call their "ontological status." They are identical *as* a Whole, and different *as* parts. The Whole corresponds to the side of identity, the part to the side of difference. And the aim is to resolve this contradiction by making the parts work together in the most rational way to form the Whole, to bring the Whole into reality, to make the Whole exist – by bringing it out of its state of just essence, just purpose. Imagine a jigsaw puzzle: the Whole is the final image that exists only in potentiality (and therefore, does not really exist) because for now, the pieces are a big messy pile – the parts. The image can *only* be formed by the pieces, and the pieces are nothing (or rather, they have no meaning) without contributing to the final image. Each can only exist through the other. When the parts are in disorder, the Whole is just an idea, and the parts have no purpose... We have the "abstract" Whole, the "bad Whole," and the "abstract" parts, the "bad parts": we have a contradiction. But when we gradually put the puzzle back together, when the parts are harmoniously arranged, we have the true Whole composed of the true parts. In politics, we would say that it is individuals who make society, while at the same time, it is the society which, when harmonious, *enables* the individuation process – there is no such thing as a happy society composed of unhappy individuals, and no such thing as happy individuals in an unhappy society... So there are three distinct things: the Whole (without the parts, still just a goal), the parts (without the Whole, the puzzle pieces in disorder and making no sense) and the Whole-Parts – synthesis of the two, the goal is achieved, the puzzle has become itself, has made sense *through* the process of rational organization of the pieces. Or again, a happy society is composed of happy individuals...

You write: "I find it hard to understand how two things could be relatively different without also being relatively the same." That is precisely what they are: in the absolute, there is only one thing, the world perfectly identical to itself. But everywhere else, in the relative parts, everything is relatively identical as well as relatively different. Hence historicity: the world tends (or can tend) towards an "identical identity" (reconciliation of the parts) or remains a Whole torn apart by differences that do not combine but clash with each other – the parts that are unaware that they are part of a whole. I will come back to this below.

On the next point: yes, if being and non-being are absolutely different, this is a specificity of this moment of Logic. They are totally foreign to each other, because they have not yet been reunited in becoming. That said, being and non-being are gigantic abstractions, in the highly abstract sphere of being. In the sphere of essence, on the other hand, the difference between one thing and another can only be relative. Moreover, the concept of difference necessarily refers to that of identity, and vice versa. This is why I would not say that being and non-being are different, but rather radically *alien* – although even this word is not enough to express this total disconnection. Being and non-being do not have the connection that being-there and being-another have... Being *disappears* into non-being, while being-there *passes* into being-another.

You want to "know to what extent the bacterium is not you" and you want to "know a way of determining this degree of difference": that is the whole point. There is no clear boundary between the self and the world. The world is what I make of it, and I am what it makes of me – at least that is the basic logical structure. Hence phrases like "How stupid those politicians are!" to which we can reply "Yes, but it is the people who vote for them!"; hence the possibility of passing the buck *ad infinitum*: "We have the leaders we deserve" but also "The leaders have the people they deserve," and so on. Or the statement: "Damned nature gave me a bacterium" can be turned into "Hey, you silly, why did not you wear a mask?"... Now why the decision on responsibility for a fault is "relative" (we look for extenuating or aggravating circumstances, etc.)? This is not because things would be "blurred." It is the very structure of the world, a fundamentally contradictory structure (hence the need for dialectics) that creates these reversals of perspective. It is not by chance or approximation that it is hard to find who to blame. It is perfectly clear that the fault is attributable to anyone, because everyone is guilty, and therefore, no one in particular is... Here I recognize (and now I understand) what you are saying about madness or silence. But there is a way out of this crisis, and only one: dialectics that lead to the "end of history." Today, there is a crime (let us say theft): right-wingers will say "punishment!" (even though it does not cancel out the crime or prevent subsequent crimes) and left-wingers will say "prevention!" – thus *justifying* theft with poverty. The only solution, however utopian it may seem, lies at the end of history, when there is no longer any reason to commit a crime. Until then, we are in a state of contradiction: everything is true and everything is false, everyone is guilty and everyone is innocent, and so on. But this is not the *absurdity* of the world; it is rather its *non-realization* (or its still incomplete realization) that gives it the *appearance* of absurdity.

So yes, the bacteria themselves are also you, not just because they are part of your body once they are inside, but also and above all *in essence* (in common essence, i.e., the Whole), just as you are *also* the Sun (you are nourished by its rays, etc.) and the Sun is also you – you bring it to life by contemplating it, absorbing its rays, talking about it... Hence the *dignity* I was talking about: all things are different, but at the same time, nothing is "superior" in the absolute. The solution to this contradiction is harmony, or the realization of the Whole *through* its parts.

It is very interesting what you say about the murderer example. You are right overall, but personally I would put it this way: if you go to war to defend your country, for example, it is suicide in the sense that you know you are risking death, but a suicide that you accept for a cause you are defending. As for the murderer who kills you, it is exactly the opposite: he has saved his life, but he has killed his spiritual life. By killing you, he has exchanged a potential human relationship for the inhuman relationship of murder, which leads to a life of shame. Admittedly, a soldier is not generally comparable to a murderer, but the idea is there. When one man kills another, the latter loses his bodily life and the former pays in another way – through shame, prison, fear of revenge... Once you have murdered a man, let us say to rob him (to put aside the "legitimacy" of defending a noble cause), you are no longer really a human being in the strongest sense of the word...

You intend to show "how the study of any particular example (murder, bacteria...) becomes complex through dialectics." I would rather say that it *passes* through a stage of complexity to gradually rise to light, to truth. Of course, the other option, that of binary thinking ("good guy" versus "bad guy," etc.) is simple and clear, but it is false – or, as Hegel would say, "abstract." It is always a matter of *self-interested* opinion, so that action, or "decidability," is easy indeed. This is when everyone defends their own interests. Everyone tries to exploit the situation unfairly. This is the "state of nature" – Hobbes' state of nature, not Rousseau's state of nature. We have to choose between being humans or beasts. Moreover, since we are (in essence) human, we *must* (categorical imperative) make the effort to rise to this complexity, this difficulty. Of course, it is difficult, and we sometimes find ourselves saying: "Actually, it may not be so bad to be a fern"...

I do not think we should give up on being human, or even honest. We do not even need to be exemplary, to succeed in changing the world. Just trying to do so is "being human." We should not hate ourselves for our weaknesses or be content to indulge them. In my text on freedom and determinism, I first wrote, before withdrawing it, in the chapter on "inclinations": "It is true that we often find ourselves saying that *between ourselves and the universal will, there is still a little room for a second slice of cake*" – let me rephrase that. Even if Marx collapses, we have Kant as a safety net against falling back on Hobbes. Because, the day you dine at Hobbes's, you realize too late that he has also invited Sade!

So yes, the theoretical and practical dialectic is difficult (its complexity is a reflection of the complexity of the world), but it is our fate as humans, the price of freedom and consciousness.

You see me "insisting that Hegel did not simply show the internal contradiction of everything (and thus the madness proper to reason and the absurdity proper to the world)." In fact, I would say that nature is indeed "crazy" (but in a non-pejorative, non-"guilty" sense) if you want to use that word, since nature is this negation of logic (negation in the sense of externalization), then elucidated and understood by reason. For me, reason is the opposite of craziness, it is the remedy, and it rediscovers logic *through* this infinite fragmentation of meaning by nature.

As for Hegel's study of the concept of limit, it seems to me that this is a step forward in analysis, because it replaces a whole movement of contradictions with a single term, a single concept. Of course, anyone who takes the *word* limit without grasping its *concept*, anyone who believes that a limit is a separation between two totally *distinct* things, has understood nothing, because he falls back (without knowing it) into pure being. The true limit, the *concept* of limit properly understood, *contains the path*, the memory, and the knowledge that the limit is the relation of contradiction between two different things that are at the same time one. In everyday language, the word "limit" is used superficially – like the word "being," for example, and like all words, in fact. And Hegel precisely wants to express the world in everyday language (without far-fetched neologisms), with simple words, but *simple words in which he reveals all the deep and hidden meanings*. But in a way you are right, often a concept simply "gathers up" the previous ones, adding very little.

Sometimes, we even stumble on a concept of logic when it only summarizes the previous steps – we cannot find it because we are looking too far. But here, the limit needs to be posited to justify the following concept, i.e., the *finite*... You describe this presentation of the limit in *Logic* as a disappointment, a kind of swindle, whereas it is actually the very proof that the method is sensible. Logic tells the world in human words – with admittedly complex interactions. Reason *breaks* the "absurdity of the world" by traversing the superficiality of words to eventually restore their deeper meaning. Another remark on this subject: I do not think that the *concept* of limit is used to construct buildings. It is used for metaphysical and political questions. For sewing or playing a football match, the *word* "limit" is enough. But if you want to think about a question like "reform or revolution," you need the *concept*.

You write: "Hegel has shown that every "something" has both a necessary link to others (its being-for-others) and a kind of core impervious to others – the being-in-itself, which makes that the something and its other are not the same thing." Be careful, here you cease for a second to "firmly maintain the contradiction," which can only lead to misunderstandings. The something is *entirely* contradiction. The something is not *composed* of a "link to others" and an "impenetrable core". No, *the something is entirely other, at the same time as it is entirely itself.* You (classic mistake) relaxed your vigilance for a second and binary understanding made an incursion into your reasoning. Understanding has quietly resurfaced to bring its principle of non-contradiction back into contradiction. Coherence must not be forced by under-standing, but must rather emerge, when the time comes, from contradiction itself, which, as it progresses, tends towards greater coherence... In this case, in logic, the initial tearing apart of being is reflected in the essence and later resolved in the *concept*.

Now I see what you mean about the madness or silence that would result from dialectics and not from understanding. I would say, however, that the blame, in this case, lies with the dialectic *of the world* – as I wrote, it is nature that does not make sense, that is "mad." The dialectic of human thought, on the other hand, strives to understand this dialectical unfolding of the world, and therefore, *contradicts* the contradiction by resolving it, at least partly – through Hegel's system or Marx's political struggle. That is why you are right, it is the *position* of the understanding that is easy and quiet (which is why it is so tempting), but the *effort* of dialectical reason remains the only real way out. A bourgeois with a comfortable life does not really *need* to think, just as a working-class person does not really have the *leisure* to do so. But really changing the world presupposes thinking, and real thinking presupposes dialectics. So you have a point: it is reason that can lead to madness – whereas understanding is actually comfortable. But reason only leads to madness if you try to reach it and do not succeed. *If you succeed*, reason does not lead to madness or absurdity, but to the peace of mind of wisdom – at least, this is the postulate of all classical philosophy, not just Hegel's. Conversely, to indulge in understanding is to live in laziness, falsity, mediocrity, and denial – in short, the "happy imbecile."

Why is there historicity? As I said at the beginning, a world that is only identical to itself (being) cannot be – a world made entirely of the same thing is unthinkable. Hence the necessity of non-being, becoming, and so on. Hence the need for logic as well, which is externalized in nature (in time and space), nature being this eruption of differences in an eternal entropic tumult. But this chaos cannot be *just* chaos.

The world is a permanent movement between more or less chaos – and more or less harmony.

The same is true of our social reality. We have successive governments, more or less violent, and therefore, also more or less gentle... The question then arises: what is the best form of government? Then we realize that we have a goal here on Earth: to identify and realize the best way to live. While billions of galaxies explode or are born around us, we here have a mission: to strive for harmony rather than chaos. Towards meaning rather than absurdity – absurdity being the simple, brutal power relations. Towards love rather than hate. Good. From the moment that this goal has been set, and we realize that it has not yet been achieved, where does that leave us? The answer is: in contradiction, or in *some degree of contradiction*. The world (or rather, in this case, our social reality) is at a given place and time (in the relativity of space and time) more or less absurd and more or less sensible. The tool that enables us to move towards greater coherence (the goal, the meaning) is first and foremost thought (theory), then its translation into action (practice). So there is our current world, where "everything is relative," where everyone has their opinion (which exasperates anyone who wants to think about the rationality of the world), and there is, at the same time, "in the absolute" of the "end of history," the prospect of a better world, more humane, more rational and more sensible. More humane because, for us humans, rationality consists in realizing our true humanity. This is what historicity is: the journey from our (relatively meaningless) animal origins to our human destiny. In the meantime, we are "alienated," i.e., in this phase of development, with its advances and regressions. We are human (in essence, since the "gift" of consciousness), but in the relative of existence (here and now), we are "relatively" human. We are humans *in the making*, humans who would benefit from living in happiness (the supreme interest) but who persist in living in war, misery, and exploitation, because they have not yet found the means to resolve the theoretical and practical problems posed by the realization of history. That is why I said last time that the only reproach we can make of dialectics is that it postpones the solution to contradictions, just as religion postpones it until the afterlife – which is progress, but we would like to see the solution right now! If we look around us now, we see contradictions and divisions everywhere, which makes rationality a "tomorrow."

Hegel explains "clearly" in logic what freedom is: the concept of freedom, the rational structure of the thing, and its general definition. Hegel can do nothing for the planning of our weekend. Just like the limit: there is the limit in the trivial sense, which is sufficient for everyday tasks, and the profound concept of limit, which requires considerable effort – it needs to be meditated on at length. I still do not know exactly what freedom is, but the more I work on it (over the years), the clearer I see it. Here, I have these famous quotes in my mind: "What is 'well-known' in general, for the very reason that it is 'well-known', is not known"[46] (Hegel) And: "What is time? If no one asks me, I know what it is. If I wish to explain it to the person who is asking, I do not know"[47](Augustine). Words like "being," "appearing," "freedom," "relative,""absolute," etc., which seem very simple and clear to us, are actually objects of meditation *for a lifetime...*

L. M.

---

[46] Hegel, *The Phenomenology of Mind*, trans. J. B. Baillie (New York: Harper, 1967), 92.
[47] Augustine, *Confessions*, Book XI.

Fourth message

The fact that the Whole must logically negate itself as a difference of parts is understandable, but the fact that it must differentiate itself into greater or lesser parts is what I wanted to see proven. A universe could "exist" with a set of equal parts, it seems to me...?

Your example of dignity is very clear, but its strength is its weakness: it is psychological, not logical. Besides, the most intuitive observation is that this hierarchy between species is above all psychologically and biologically founded. For example, you save the baby rather than the animal because you are biologically determined to do so. It is a biological selfishness. Similarly, an animal would save its young first before saving man, unless it has been conditioned by man. This animal's hierarchy of species would not be yours, so there would be nothing objective about Hegel's hierarchy. This reminds me of Plato's *Statesman*, where the Stranger imagines that, if the crane were to classify and rank animals, it would set itself apart from all the others, the "wild beasts," to glorify itself[48].

Not to mention the historically and sociologically grounded nature of the term "dignity," as well as its vagueness – does a ten-week-old fetus have dignity? and so on.

You write: "It is the Sun that allows life, but it is life that enables the Sun to make itself useful to life." I agree, but

---

[48] Plato, *Statesman*, 263c-d.

the difference in terms of power between the Sun and me has yet to be shown logically – in short, I still ask myself this question of the more and the less, whereas the equal could be so in quality *and* quantity. But maybe Hegel does not demonstrate this, because for him it is a matter of contingency. Just like when he considers it impossible (and pointless) to demonstrate the existence of Krug's fountain pen, because it would be contingent. In short, everything is demonstrable, except what Hegel deems indemonstrable.

Indeed, on the subject of pure being and nothingness, this is probably a specific feature of the beginning of the *Logic*.

You also write: "But this is not the absurdity of the world; it is rather its non-realization (or its still incomplete realization) that gives it the appearance of absurdity." This, then, is the fundamental point to explain: the fact that there is not a non-realization of meaning, but a nonsense that tries to become a sense. It needs to be proven that there is a tendency towards rationalization, an effort to overcome contradiction. To underpin this, we could look at history as Hegel sometimes does, noting how empires became democracies, etc., but this progress would remain highly debatable – new forms of exploitation today, threats of human extinction... Hegel himself acknowledges that we may never achieve this goal. So, what then prevents us from adding: maybe it is because there is not even a tendency to achieve this goal? That there is an effort to rationalize the world, and that it is particularly present in human beings, I have no doubt whatsoever about it, but it is highly doubtful that there is more than a mere effort, a vain agitation, in short, a Sisyphean task.

Your answer to the murder example is also interesting. It now remains to prove it, and that does not look very easy, it seems to me. "When one man kills another, the latter loses his bodily life and the former pays in another way." As you can see, this implies a kind of dualism. The chain of material effects would be cut off from the chain of spiritual effects. The murderer loses *only* what I brought him spiritually, while he also took away my bodily life and depended on it *too* – the limit of his body depended on the limit of mine. He totally won the "bodily battle" while he partially lost the "spiritual battle."

Moreover, this partial loss of the "spiritual battle" for the murderer must be qualified. He may have no remorse (like some of the convicts described by Dostoyevsky), escape prison, have no fear of vengeance... As for the recognition I gave him through my consciousness, which he has now lost, he can quickly go and find it in one of the billions of other available human beings. Whereas I have lost *everything*. So, it is always the same problem: the results are extremely unequal, while we were both entirely relative to each other, on a physical and spiritual level, we were unfailingly linked.

The fact that I have "lost everything," by the way, raises a very interesting (and problematic) question about death in the Hegelian system, about the passage to non-being. If every thing is linked to everything else, if everything is a system, how can we understand that the disappearance of one thing does not trigger the disappearance of everything? This brings to my mind a rather strong argument about what we were talking about earlier: not only is the tendency towards the unity of the Whole, the logical progress towards unity, hardly perceptible and remains to be demonstrated but, what is more, the success of this project could be the worst-case scenario because, when everything is organically connected, the disappearance of one part may lead to the disappearance of all the others. You will notice that I am talking about an organic Whole, not a rigid Whole that is always identical to itself, as in Parmenides or Spinoza – since Hegel has this organic Whole in mind. With Spinoza or Parmenides, it is obvious that nothing can disappear without the disappearance of the Whole, and that is why nothing disappears – it is just an illusion of the senses, to make a long story short. But when a part of the organic Whole disappears, it is no joy either: if my heart disappears, my whole body disappears. The only solution would be to say that my whole body disappears (if my heart disappears) because it is not organic enough. It is organic enough to survive the disappearance of certain parts: the disappearance of my kidney or my lung will lead to a very significant adaptation of my body, but by virtue of its plasticity, my body will adapt and continue to live. So Hegel would say that the universe tends to become a perfectly organic, perfectly "plastic" whole. This remains to be demonstrated – see above.

You say that dialectics only "go through" a stage of complexity. But I do not see the next stage, the stage where it becomes clear enough for action. Hence the fact that, after a while, I refuse to say that this is simply a weakness of our intellects: rather, it is a characteristic of reality itself. I propose to say that truth is nothing other than this complexity hindering decision.

You suggest that only nature is crazy. You refuse to say "guilty," yet it does sound like you are doing what you criticized earlier: passing the buck. It also resembles what Hegel said about Krug's pen.

Regarding the notion of "limit," which I believe could conceal the pain of contradiction rather than overcome it (and would therefore only be a word, not a new concept), I am not sure how solid your answer is. You continue to argue that there is an act of overcoming, a result, a *destination* containing the journey, and not just the repetition of the journey or the juxtaposition of stages. But this remains to be proven. According to you, there is a step and a destination. As I see it, there are two elements (being-in-itself and being-for-others) wrapped up in purely linguistic wrapping paper – or at least we can raise that suspicion.

You also refer to the discovery of the limit in *Logic* as "the very proof that the approach makes sense," but I do not see where the proof is. I repeat: we use the concept of limit peacefully in everyday life because we forget that it is contradictory. To help you answer this objection, you could suggest (this would be rather unprovable and would look like an *ad hoc* hypothesis, but effective): the concept of limit is more than a contradiction, it is an overcoming and not a return to the alleged confusion of the world, as evidenced by the fact that everyone uses it every day in a constructive and practical way, *even though they do not know the truth of this concept*: actually, if they can build so successfully from it, it must be because they *unconsciously* know the constructive truth of this concept. But if we start saying that all the contradictions of Hegelian logic are overcome unconsciously...

"To think about a question like 'reform or revolution,' you need the *concept*." Yes, but is the concept available? Do we have more than a word at our disposal? That is the question.

"You (classic mistake) relaxed your vigilance for a second and the binary understanding made an incursion into your reasoning." Maybe, my mistake. But then it seems to me that Hegel himself goes back and forth between binary and dialectical thinking in his *Logic*. Because, how can we show that there is a *unification* of two concepts without saying, at least temporarily, that these two concepts are non-unified? Any unification presupposes the unification of two things that are not initially unified, or at least presented as such. Hegel's way out, it seems to me, is to speak not of two sides of a concept, but of two "pairs" or "moments." Example: the chapter on Being-there, B. a. 2: "Being-for-another and being-in-itself constitute the *two moments* of something. These are *two pairs* of determinations that meet here." Perhaps this is a vain terminological trick, because, even when he says "two pairs" of the same thing, there is still a "two," a differentiation. Two "moments," this is still a binary thought, a thought of understanding! Through which Hegel tries to express this dialectic...but is it precisely expressible? I will say it again: generally speaking, I often have the impression when reading the *Logic* (at least its beginning) that Hegel is painfully revolving around something *inexpressible*. It is as if I were reading: "These two concepts are one, but do not forget that there are two, but do not forget that they are one..."

Hegel does indeed describe a being-in-itself of the something, impervious to the other. But why does he talk about it, if only to immediately add that it is somehow stupid, because the something is, in fact, entirely other? He does so gratuitously, and for a simple and good reason: if he always just "held contradiction firmly," *Logic* could not move forward. You have to bring in differentiations that are presented as real, and not simply as the other side of identity, otherwise you never get beyond the initial confusion of pure being and nothingness... And I do think that Hegel never really goes beyond that! I believe that there is no real progress in the *Science of Logic* (no overcoming), that you have to open this book anywhere and then read it *backward*: to see that, in fact, everything always comes back to confusion ("absurdity") of the pure being which is nothingness and the other way around. *Science of Logic* is all about grasping that our rationality is based on nothing. Now I understand why A. was thinking of Wittgenstein. *Science of Logic* should be read in the same way as the *Tractatus*: "My propositions serve as elucidations in the following way: anyone who understands me eventually recognizes them as nonsensical (...)" The comparison with Wittgenstein, however, has its limits:

Wittgenstein believes that it is possible to "overcome" (überwinden) this nonsense to "see the world correctly" (richtig). I think, on the contrary, that there is a simplification, and that only to act.

About this tendency towards harmony, progress, and wisdom, I would again express doubt and ask for proof of this tendency. However, it is likely that, if we had proof of the existence of this path leading to harmony and wisdom, we would take it. You might not have such proof for that reason. Then we would simply have to stop arguing and "wait" for the course of history to prove one of us right... Even so, this verdict could never be in my favor, because even if the absurdity persisted, it would still be possible to hope and imagine that the rational destination exists but has not yet been reached.

You write: "If we succeed, reason does not lead to madness or absurdity, but to the peace of mind of wisdom – at least, this is the postulate of all classical philosophy, not just Hegel's." Absolutely, it is a *postulate*. Until Nietzsche and Freud arrived.

I read the end of your message with attention and interest. It seems to me that it is conditioned by elements already mentioned above, so I will not say more.

L. F.

Fourth Response

A universe could not exist with a set of equal parts. First of all, it would be an extraordinary "coincidence," a bit like throwing a billion matches into the air and having them fall to the ground perfectly aligned and parallel... But, above all, and more seriously, it is the very nature of the difference to be unequal. The world is unequal because it cannot be otherwise: how can we imagine a world where man is as big as a planet (or the planet as big as the system that contains it)? For that matter, a human thumb would also need to be as big as the whole human, and so on. I do not think there is any point in asking why things are different (in size, in power), because the opposite is strictly unthinkable... And the issue of difference (like the energy difference between you and the Sun) is actually a question for science. From a logical point of view, I do not see any problem.

Dignity is a psychological notion, *but it is the psychological application of the logical concept* of the Whole. I "descend" into the psychological realm to illustrate the logic from which it necessarily comes. But you are right about this: the hierarchy between the human and the animal is entirely human. We can even imagine aliens on other planets, who must surely consider themselves to be the pinnacle of creation and who would regard us as aliens – possibly edible... Hierarchies are relative and self-interested, but they do exist – just like the ultimate goal of "dignity," "harmony between species," exists in the background. But I still wonder: is not there an objective hierarchy, I mean the *hierarchy of consciousness* (or, if you like, the hierarchy between the lifeless and the living being)? I am not sure that, in a building in flames, the coffee pot would choose to save the toaster... Or rather, a better example: if the crane were *capable* of classifying and ranking animals, it would quite *rightly* set itself apart from all the others.

Without getting into a debate on abortion, I would say that the fetus obviously has dignity to the extent that I consider even lifeless things to have it: the soup tureen has a "dignity" insofar as it is (among other things) crystallized human labor. It is, therefore, in a way, composed of human activity, albeit "past" human. Hence the discomfort we feel when confronted with waste, with the idea of throwing away something "that can still be used." But that does not mean that the soup tureen will not be "saved last"; and we must keep in mind that, alongside the dignity of the fetus, there is the dignity of the woman, who also has the right to make autonomous decisions about her body, and so on – hence the debate...

To relate this to what has just been said, it can be argued that the universe does not care whether we live or die, whether we move towards democracy or dictatorship, and so on. And, to answer a point you make later on, I am not sure that, on a cosmic level, the universe is looking for unity... Perhaps this tendency towards unity is desired by living species, locally, for example on Earth. But, as *living* beings, endowed with consciousness and sensitivity (capacity for pleasure, pain), we have a real *interest* to move towards the good – or, to respect the relativity of hierarchy, towards what is good *for man*. Therefore, the meaning of history is not a mechanism, but our choice: do we want to live cleanly or not? Do we want to eat our fill or be starving? Do we want to live in tenderness and friendship, or violence and fear? Nothing is written in advance, and our good may not be the good of alien X on planet Y, but the fact is that it is in our interest to move towards good rather than evil – more than an obvious statement, it is a tautology, to say so. There must be some better ways of living (respect, harmony...) and some less good ways – neurosis, violence... Having said that, I am not even claiming that one government is better than another (that is up for discussion), but there is bound to be a *meaning* that we have to find – unless we are saying that everything is the same: rape and love, sickness and health... And it is up to us to find this meaning. We only speak of the "self-movement" of history to the extent that, man being the extension of nature, we can also consider (this is the point of view of the Whole), that nature realizes itself when we realize ourselves. There is a "trend," but this trend is nothing more than our own *efforts*. I would add that, while from a scientific point of view, progress is obvious, it is more debatable from a philosophical and political point of view. But I do believe that a great deal has been achieved so far (for example, in the history of France, the introduction of social security and free schooling are certainly examples of progress) and that parts of the puzzle have already been put together, giving us reason to believe in the "final picture."

My idea of "spiritual death" (used to keep insisting on equality which, admittedly, is not obvious) is perhaps far-fetched. I am just trying to push reasoning to the limit – the reasoning of the dialectic of master and slave, both responsible for the struggle, both linked in their destiny and, more generally, the Hegelian reasoning about the whole and the parts... In fact, it is always very difficult to defend, because you are always looking for the extreme example (which is legitimate), such as murder. It is reminiscent of Voltaire, who mocked Leibniz's theodicy with great humor but also in an oversimplified way: Leibniz is not an idiot who thinks that war is a good thing. He is an intelligent man who points out the following fact: once you have said that war is bad, you have not said anything at all! I wonder whether an answer to our problem might not be this: by virtue of the fact that man is not just himself (the individual) but is "himself-in-the-world," perhaps theodicy is in fact true only in the collective – in the whole. In other words, whatever happens, *humanity* gets what it deserves. But when we look at the details of individuals, we see bad guys winning, good guys losing, and so on. Hegel talks about this in *Reason in History*: it is easy to deplore individual misery or even collective misery *at one point in history*, while overlooking the work of the positive through the negative, over the long term and for the whole of humanity.

On the last point: "If every thing is linked to everything else, if everything is a system, how can we understand that the disappearance of one thing does not lead to the disappearance of everything else?" In fact, nothing disappears, everything is transformed... For the cosmos, it makes no difference whether we are a living body or a corpse that feeds the beasts. The energy of our atoms persists... But for us, of course, it makes a difference... As for Hegel's organic whole, once again, the existence of the whole as a whole in no way precludes hierarchies – the fact that, for you, your heart is more important than your foot, and your foot more important than your hair, and so on.

As for the complexity of dialectics, this is the classic criticism. Moreover, since the solution to the contradictions has not yet been found, the effectiveness of dialectics is doubtful. It is a bit of a leap of faith – I will come back to that.

The limit is a concept that is a step forward, although again, once you have understood it, you think it is simple, not a big deal. We had two things related to each other. The limit is the grasp of the whole relation – this grasp is one. The limit is not a line that separates two things or brings them together: in the limit we understand that we can make the two things disappear, because they are in fact contained in the concept of limit, properly understood. According to you, there is no progress when we go from being and non-being to becoming? In that case, each concept is just wrapping paper for the previous one, and the whole logic is just a series of Russian dolls that contain nothing but themselves! That is not entirely untrue, by the way, since logic does indeed have that circular nature which, while unfolding, unfolds nothing other than what it contains from the beginning...

You write: "But then it seems to me that Hegel himself goes back and forth between binary and dialectical thinking in his *Logic*. Because how can we show that there is a unification of two concepts without speaking, at least temporarily, of these two concepts as non-unified?" *Absolutely*, he does it all the time. In fact, he is obliged to show each time the abstract point of view as it turns out to be contradictory, to then explain its overcoming.

"It is as if I were reading: 'These two concepts are one, but do not forget that there are two, but do not forget that they are one...'" Again, true, but perfectly logical! The whole logic (and the whole system) is a headlong rush that finds no solution (or not until the end) so that each concept is both the (dialectical) synthesis of previous moments *and* the abstract moment for the next synthesis to come – so here it is a non-dialectical moment. That is why it is so difficult to read: there is this double perspective all the time – it is also the "for us" and the "for consciousness" that we see everywhere in the *Phenomenology of Spirit*. We should not forget, by the way, that dialectics is the overcoming-*preservation* of binary thinking; dialectics relies on the binary, it needs it. The binary is not false, it is just incomplete. The binary only becomes "false" when we do not dialecticize it.

The contradiction of the beginning (being, nothingness) remains throughout the logic, but is deepened and enriched. There is total contradiction in being and non-being, where everything collapses. Then, in phenomenon and thing-in-itself, in effect and cause, etc., there is still contradiction, but everything that comes before is perfectly grounded – and therefore, no longer really contradictory. Every new concept deals with contradiction. I think you are missing the point that there is more than pure coherence and pure contradiction: contradictions are relative, more or less contradictory, and that is what progress is all about. The simple fact of knowing, once we have arrived at the essence, that being is in fact contradictory, is already a victory, if not a solution – we now have the *knowledge* of contradiction, then the knowledge of new contradictions, and so on. Of course, it is not the complete solution. If we were to give up on Hegel because he did not explain *everything*, then we would have to throw all the other philosophers out with the bathwater – starting with Wittgenstein, perhaps, who speaks up to say that we should keep quiet. Should we go on hunger strike just because we do not understand all that is involved in the process of eating?

Strictly speaking, I would not say that nature is crazy (I used that word since you mentioned it), but rather that nature only makes sense to the consciousness that grasps that meaning. It makes sense (the sense that is already here "in itself") only with consciousness. That is why it is logical that nature can *appear* absurd, but it is precisely the role of the mind to find this lost meaning. All this stems, in fact, from a Hegelian postulate of reason. For example, Hegel might say: madness is the loss of reason; therefore, for madness to exist, the world must be rational! I am willing to admit that this does not prove anything, as the postulate is self-supporting. You ask for proof... But then I ask you: prove to me that the world is absurd. That is what I said about freedom and determinism: you ask for proof of freedom, but you never ask for proof of determinism!

There is indeed a kind of leap of faith in the idea that dialectics finally "resolves itself" (the historicity of philosophy and that of the political world), but it is by seeing the progression of the concept (such as that of limit) that we can "reasonably" (if not rationally) assume that everything makes sense. That is why the reproach leveled at Hegelian dialectics, which seems acceptable to me, is not that of being senseless, but that of having a meaning that is postponed: there is some faith here that comes to mingle with philosophy. You are free not to believe it, but doubt, skepticism, Wittgenstein, etc., do not prove anything either. Hegel is no more fragile then, but perhaps more optimistic. I believe that in philosophy you never prove anything (and I am not sure that even in science you can), but you argue. Hegel seems to me to be only the most profound in his argumentation. Everything I hear from the proponents of "doubt" and "absurdity," I find it very unconvincing. But maybe it is a choice. Maybe deep down I *want* the world to be coherent. But who is to say it is not you who wants it not to be? This act of faith of mine consists in taking the path of goodwill, of hope.

I wrote that "reason does not lead to madness or absurdity but, on the contrary, to the peace of mind of wisdom – in any case, this is the postulate of all classical philosophy, not just Hegel's." Actually, I am a bit wrong here. In classical philosophy, there are already skeptics. You answer: "Absolutely, it is a postulate. Until Nietzsche and Freud arrived." Exactly, and Nietzsche and Freud formulate postulates *too...*

L. M.

Fifth message

Of course, a world made up of equal parts would be extraordinary, but I was aiming precisely at the theoretical aspect of the matter. I do not see why it would be theoretically impossible. A mathematician can very well imagine a square cut into four equal parts. Just as in physics we may one day realize that the universe is made up of particles of equal size. If you look at the world on a subatomic scale, it already seems less unimaginable that the universe could be made up of equal parts.

You write: "Dignity is a psychological notion, but it is the psychological application of the logical concept of the Whole." In that case, I would like to know the real demonstration, without the psychological detour. In short, what I asked for before. For I cannot be satisfied with the postulate that the psychological realm "necessarily comes from logic."

You also write: "I would say that the fetus obviously has a dignity insofar as I consider that even lifeless things have it." In this case, your extreme extension of the concept of dignity destroys the concept of dignity. If everything has dignity, then nothing does, yet dignity consists precisely in granting a higher status to what is worthy, compared to other things. You also seem to assume the existence of "more" or "less" dignified things, but here again, this would destroy the concept of dignity, which assumes the equality of all dignified beings. Dignity is either total or it is not.

I read that "the meaning of history is not a mechanism" but rather "our choice." However, this does not seem to answer my question. As a reminder: "This, then, is the fundamental point to explain: the fact that there is not a non-realization of meaning, but a nonsense trying to become sense." Whether or not the tendency to make sense of the world is our choice does not answer my question. An individual can very well choose to strive to see meaning in the world (and I believe that every individual does it) without the world actually making any sense, and therefore, without this individual's effort being rewarded. I do not think it can ever be rewarded, since this effort is an epiphenomenon whose purpose is to mask the fundamental meaninglessness of the world. As for the proof of this fundamental nonsense of the world, my position from the beginning has been that Hegel provides this proof, by showing that everything, ultimately, is conditioned by the contradiction of pure being and nothingness. You choose to read the *Science of Logic* starting from the beginning, with unshakeable confidence in its "progress," whereas I propose to read it in reversed order, to see that everything rests on an unsurmountable contradiction. And I have tried to show that this reading is possible by expressing a strong suspicion of the "surpassing" value of each logical moment of the book.

"There is bound to be a *meaning*": once again, where is the proof? It seems you are just trying to convince yourself here. You seem to categorically reject the hypothesis that all this might not make sense. If you cannot suppose that possibility, I understand why you cannot subscribe to it.

You also write: "For the cosmos, it is indifferent whether we are a living body or a corpse that feeds the beasts." I find this idea rather surprising for a Hegelian, since, in Hegel's view, nature itself has a destiny closely linked to that of human consciousness. I am not so sure that "for the cosmos, it is irrelevant whether we are a living body or a corpse," given that if all conscious beings disappear, it is not certain that for Hegel the cosmos continues to exist. For a Hegelian, it seems to me that it would be regrettable if the cosmos could no longer hope to become conscious of itself through the intermediary of humans.

"The limit is the understanding of the whole relation – this understanding is one." What we can be sure of is that it is grasping the *contradiction* in its entirety. But the presence of the word "limit" does not solidly establish a healthy "relation" for contradiction. "This understanding is one," but this unity could only be linguistic and not conceptual, in short, concealment of the contradiction and not its "overcoming." On this point, I have the impression that we have reached a dialogue of the deaf. Where I allow myself to express suspicions, you refuse to do the same in the name of "faith." But if it is a question of faith, your videos are more proselytism than philosophy.

Furthermore, you sometimes support what I am saying, but this makes what you were saying earlier problematic. I am thinking of the following: you criticized my use of a "binary" way of thinking, and now you approve of it, pointing out that Hegel himself uses it in his exposition and, what is more, preserves it in his "overcoming." From then on, the criticism you leveled at me faded, and I legitimately referred to a "core impervious to others" that each thing has. You said to me: "You (classic mistake) relaxed your vigilance for a second and binary understanding made an incursion into your reasoning." But now we see that this was no mistake since binary understanding is preserved in dialectics. However, you see this moment of binary thinking as something non-essential that logically leads to the "overcoming." I am not convinced of this "overcoming," as I have tried to show.

You describe the act of "knowing that being is in fact contradictory" as constituting a "victory." But you cannot *know* a contradiction, you cannot make something out of it, you cannot build on contradiction... In short, we keep coming back to the idea of an "overcoming" that, in my opinion, does not exist. The *Science of Logic* brings the contradiction of the world to light, but at the same time hides this discovery.

"If we were to give up on Hegel because he did not explain *everything*...": Hegel did not explain everything, but he did claim to explain the everything, the whole. What is more, I am not saying that we should give up on Hegel, but just that we should read him from a non-Hegelian point of view.

You point out that "doubt and skepticism (...) prove *nothing* either." But precisely, thanks to Hegel, nonsense is rigorously proven. However, I do agree that we can do nothing with this proof since it is nonsense. If you are looking for useful, optimistic knowledge, you will have to turn to the false and simplified, to science or religion – which is what everybody does, more or less. But I think it is good to be reminded *once in a while* of the absurd truth of the world, for reasons I will not expand on here. I would also like to comment on this simplification: Hegel helps to counter an objection that has been made to Nietzsche. I will summarize it as follows: "Our thoughts are simplifications... but simplifications of what? Logically: simplifications of something that is not yet simplified and that we can grasp." And with Hegel, we know what our thoughts are simplifications of: they are simplifications of the contradictory truth of the world.

You are assuming that I am the one who wants the world to be absurd and incoherent. It is possible, but unlikely, for two reasons. First of all, in my opinion, Hegel already proved it, so it is not simply my wish. Secondly, awareness of the absurdity of the world would not be of much interest to me: it is not exactly reassuring and it does not help life much – hence the idea of approaching it "once in a while." Could I use it to relieve myself of responsibility? "Since nothing makes sense, I feel responsible for nothing"? I cannot even adopt this attitude, since it makes no more sense to feel responsible than not to feel responsible. I have also noted on several occasions that I, like almost all of humankind, would like the world not to be absurd; for this reason, I very frequently forget the contradictory truth of the world, or at least I often prefer Democritus' laughter to Heraclitus' tears.

By way of conclusion, I would like to emphasize one last time that I am not throwing out Hegel's philosophy. In fact, first of all, his philosophy is the "demonstration of absurdity," so to speak. Secondly, many elements of his philosophy shed light on our world – for example, the dialectic of master and slave, which helps us to understand certain human relationships. However, these elements only help us if we allow them a certain degree of simplification. For, if we take their truth to its logical conclusion, we get the opposite of what we were aiming for: we get the undecidable and the unspeakable. You reach the absurd depths of reality. I am well aware that we cannot *do* much with the interpretation I have defended. However, it relegates the idea of dialectical progress to the status of an object of faith, and, all in all, this is not insignificant, because then we are allowed to think elsewhere and we escape the impression that dialectics absorbs everything different from it.

Thank you for these discussions,


L. F.

Fifth Response

I agree, but if you look at the subatomic scale, the answer is easy: the parts are equal, and the Sun is bigger (or has more energy, etc.) because it is made up of many more parts than you.

You are asking for a purely logical demonstration or proof that the psychological fact necessarily follows from logic. However, the real (attempted) demonstration I gave earlier was about the whole and the parts. Since I could not make myself understood, I used an example.

Regarding dignity, it is the side (*of the contradiction*) by which things are equal (in which they are the Whole) and, faced with this, there are the possible hierarchies of the parts – hierarchies that are also necessary but that have an interest in tending to harmony. I have attempted a dialectical presentation, but it seems to me that you are still reading it in a binary way. You explain that, in my opinion, all things have dignity, but some have more than others. I am rather saying that all things have dignity, that they are equal in dignity, and that dignity is the only angle from which things are equal... On all other criteria, they are unequal, hence the hierarchies. Then again, perhaps my example (dignity) is not a very good one to illustrate the dialectics of whole and parts.

As I see it, you start again and again from the "fundamental nonsense of the world" (so, a postulate) to refute the idea that the world would make sense... You also say that you "have a strong suspicion about the 'overcoming' value of each logical moment of the *Science of Logic*." I agree that a suspicion is legitimate. I too have my doubts. But, if you propose *suspicions*, you should not then ask your interlocutor for *proof* of his own thesis...

I do not know if I "chose" to read this book starting from the first pages. Spontaneously, I started at the beginning... Indeed, if you read a book in reversed order, you can make it say the opposite of what it says, without a doubt... A bit like how scissors are nonsense if you hold them upside down. Jokes aside, I hear your thesis, I understand its possibility, but it is rather you who *choose* to read the book upside down. I too have tried to argue, in a way, that it should be read starting from the first pages to avoid misunderstandings. For example, it is not *at the end* of the book that something is conditioned by the contradiction of being and nothingness. On the contrary, it is so *at the beginning*. *Ultimately*, everything is conditioned by the *absolute*, which is precisely the solution to the contradiction.

If you take my statement out of context ("There has to be a meaning"), it does indeed give the impression that I am a fanatical believer. And I admit that I certainly need to believe it, because of some feelings. But every philosophical act contains feelings if philosophy is truly the *"love* of wisdom." And, I repeat, you postulate as much as I do: since Hegel does not give you irrefutable proof of the meaning of the world (without you "proving" that he has not), you prefer to postulate that the world has no meaning (unproven thesis) as if the burden of proof must necessarily fall on the other.

You write that a logical unit (moments of progress) "could only be linguistic, not conceptual." However, the concept is language. It is language (that strives to be) radical. I do not mind voicing my suspicions and, above all, I fully accept that others are more suspicious than I am, or that others have other doubts than mine. I will say it: Hegel may ultimately be wrong. But he seems to me to be more radical and coherent than his opponents. That is why I place (for the time being) more faith in him. You place your faith elsewhere, fine. But doubt is an act of faith too, because, since doubt is unbearable (if it is taken seriously all the time), it sends you back to the "useful" knowledge you are talking about – science, religion. My videos are not proselytizing (and why should not they, actually?) but they are an attempted popularization. I am sorry you do not find them to your liking. They're mainly of interest to people who do not know anything about Hegel and want to find an introduction – one has to explain Hegel's point of view before considering refuting it.

The "impervious core" of the something is a *moment* (the moment of binary abstraction), binary thinking is a moment of the dialectic, it is indeed overcome, but overcome-preserved. You made this mistake the first time and you are repeating it here. You inject here and there the binary into dialectics, or the other way around, and then you are surprised to find it all contradictory when you need to understand the precise and rational nature of their connections. You would like to choose between binary and dialectical thinking (or find a bit of both where you like), whereas the latter stems from the former to resolve its contradiction – the binary and the dialectical thinking are a moment of each other, and form a whole. This solution is, at a given moment, only partial, but it is still a step forward. Well, if I failed to convince you of that, I will not now.

This may not invalidate your final point and your general view of Hegel, but you speak of dialectics with too much imprecision to, in my opinion, be able to refute it. But then again, maybe, *in the end,* you are right. I often wonder if I am not the one who underestimates (due to lack of understanding) the depth, for example, of Nietzsche...

You write that we cannot "know contradiction, we cannot make something of it, build on it." We can already know that it is pointless to build on the binary thinking – and I think that is a huge step forward. Moreover, knowing *in what terms* essence is contradictory allows us to better situate things in relation to it... In fact, I think that whatever we do, we are always building on contradiction. Consciously or unconsciously.

You also argue that contradiction must be simplified so that humans can act. "Because, if we take the truth [of dialectics] to its logical conclusion, we get the opposite of what we were aiming for: we get the undecidable and the unspeakable." However, I do not see how simplifying the unspeakable or the absurd would produce anything other than the absurd or the arbitrary...

Regarding Hegel who would "rigorously prove nonsense," with several days' hindsight, I think I understand a little better what you are trying to tell me. You are using Hegel against Hegel, which actually does more than certain skeptics who think they're contradicting him by ignoring him altogether, or by simply declaring that "it is not true." It took me a while to understand because I had not considered this point of view. It is very interesting. However, although I will have to think about it, I do not think I would subscribe to that... I still do not think Hegel says the world is incoherent. I still believe that, on the contrary, Hegel mentions its coherence, through the deciphering (admittedly gradual, and therefore, not yet complete) of its contradictory appearance. Of course, I will never be able to prove this to you, just as you will not be able to prove the contrary to me. But, in the absence of proof, in terms of argumentation, I am still waiting for someone more convincing than Hegel...

Finally, you write: "In my opinion, Hegel proved [the absurdity of the world], so it is not simply my wish." But you are following the sense of the reader who chooses to read the book in the reverse order, so it is still your preference... You have to choose between "in my opinion" and "a proof".

After a while, it becomes, indeed, a dialogue of the deaf. Discussing like this, in writing, is very difficult. At the very least, I hope we have learned something from each other. In the end, it may not be a dialogue of the deaf: it is not (always) that we do not understand each other, it is rather that we do not agree... And that is okay. I will try to meditate on your point of view for some more time.

Thank you for these discussions,

L. M.

*End of the dialogue*

# Contents

Cover art: Ian Parker (modified)

ISBN: 978-2-9582456-3-4
editions.skhedia@gmail.com
122 rue Mouffetard, 75005 Paris, France
*Dépôt légal*: February 2024
Printed in January 2024
by Amazon KDP